Life Lessons from a Rescue Dog

By

M. J. Miller

Illustrated by Jason Barnett

To Suki and Simon

The Best Ones Ever

Contents

Acknowledgments

First, I want to thank you, the reader. Without you there'd be no point. So thank you for picking up this book and taking the time to read it. You've given me a precious gift—your time—and I don't take that for granted. Your feedback and encouragement makes me a better writer.

The first-look award again goes to Suki Brannan who sees my manuscript in its rawest form. I wouldn't dare show it to anyone else. Your support also gives me guilt-free time with the computer on "writing days." Thanks for hanging in there, my friend.

Dr. Amy Nickels, DVM has also been a great support for Simon and for Suki and me. Thank you for your excellent care and advice for our pack. (Simon sends a tail-wag.)

Thank you, Sonia Johnson, for your great suggestions—and for loving Simey, too.

Of course, I can't say enough about Scott and Sandi Tompkins—friends, mentors, editors and all-around fun people. You're both brilliant and greatly loved.

Next, I would like to thank my writer's group and those readers and wordsmiths who brought their expertise into the mix. Your faithfulness and input have kept me on track.

Finally, a big thank you to my prayer partners. You've been with me from the beginning and I know your prayers have made a difference.

Praise for *Life Lessons from the Hive*

"M. J. Miller's great instinct transforms the book into an experience, rather than just a list of insights. Well done." Judge, 25th Annual Writer's Digest Self-Published Book Awards

"A beautiful book, full of advice, instruction and encouragement." — Author, Cherie Jobe

"The way M. J. Miller has compared the body of Christ to the workings of a beehive is brilliant. — Rev. Jonathan Osterhaus

"M. J. Miller carries the reader from close understanding of bees to a deeper understanding of life with Jesus." — Author, Twink DeWitt

Chapter 1 – Coming Home

"The gift which I am sending you is called a dog, and is in fact the most precious and valuable possession of mankind."—Theodorus Gaza

"You can't live on a farm without a farm dog," my friend Janie declared as she stood on the front porch surveying the property like a real estate appraiser.

I wouldn't have called our seven-acre spread a "farm." It's more like a farmette or a country house with a sizable yard.

My ministry partner, Suki Brannan, and I had recently bid farewell to our lives in overseas work with Youth With A Mission and said, "hello" to a new life in the hills of middle Tennessee. We had purchased a house to continue our ministry and were adapting to country living. In fact, we were still unpacking when Janie, a one-woman pet rescue crusader, stopped by.

Before we knew what had happened, Bailey, a two-year-old blond Labrador-mutt mix, had moved in. With long legs and almond eyes, she was a real beauty by dog standards—and ours. She had been neglected by her previous owners and matchmaker Janie decided we had the perfect home for her. Within days Suki and Bailey bonded like long-lost relatives at a family reunion.

We had settled into a routine with Bailey, when six months later, Janie stopped by the house again with photos of a new homeless pup. "You need another dog to keep Bailey company."

"No, we don't."

"Just take a look," She purred as she shoved a photo into my hands.

A puppy—with his head cocked to the side gazed into the camera as if to say, "Won't you take me home?"

Janie knew how to set the hook. She immediately personalized him saying, "His name is Simon and he's desperate for a good home." The sub-text was: "Who knows what hardships await this adorable innocent thing if you don't rescue him."

Not again. Janie had already tried to fix us up with two cats before talking us into rescuing Bailey. I was beginning to dread seeing her car come up the drive.

"Why don't you come out to my house tomorrow? You can meet him." Janie smiled like she was flirting with a prom date.

Honestly, I don't know why we went.

Janie was sitting on the tailgate of her truck cuddling the puppy as we drove up. She held his paw in her right hand and "they" waved a welcome. We were doomed.

"This is Simon."

We looked down at the blond bundle who greeted us with a wagging tail that wiggled his whole body. I smiled. I mean who could resist a furball who greeted you like you were the one person he'd been waiting for his whole life?

"He's the last of a litter that needs a home. He's part Labrador and he's had all his shots. Here," she handed him to me. "Hold him."

"We already have Bailey," Suki resisted. "What if they don't get along?"

"Bailey will love Simon. She's grown and he's a puppy. She'll adopt him like he was her own." Janie had an answer for all our objections. "Labs are great dogs. They're loving and friendly—and smart. He won't be any trouble at all."

Of course not.

The little bundle of fur licked my chin and his big brown eyes seemed to be smiling. "Simon's a good name," I admitted as I handed him to Suki and he settled into her arms.

She rubbed the white blaze on Simon's forehead as she looked him over. "He's got freckles on his feet."

"And under his chin," I added.

"We think his father was a Blue Heeler," Janie said. "They're very smart dogs."

"I used to have a cat named Simon," Suki reflected.

"Here's a leash," Janie smiled like an agent closing the deal.

I held Simon in my lap as Suki drove home. She looked at me. "What did we just do?"

The soft pup fidgeted in my lap. "I hope he and Bailey will get along," I said.

"He'll have to stay outside."

The furball whined and fidgeted again. "I know." I rubbed the wiggler's head as I tried to ease his restlessness. "It's okay, Simey (his new pet name). We'll be home soon."

Simon gave me a confused look. He was in a different car, on an unfamiliar road, with new smells and strange people. An uncertain future awaited him and he seemed anxious.

I rubbed his head again as I tried to keep him contained. In response, Simon looked at me, stood up, made a tight turn, arched his back, heaved and threw up on my jeans!

"Not a great start," I groaned. Suki grinned. "Welcome home, little Simey-Boy."

Janie was right. After the sniffing dance which dogs perform when they meet for the first time, Bailey accepted Simon. Within half a day they were best friends and our new puppy was following Bailey around like she was his real mother.

Simon was smart, too. He quickly learned the dog pen was his domain and settled into his new house with the enthusiasm of a college student moving into his first apartment. Once he and

Bailey had established the canine code of eating etiquette, he was home and all uncertainty was gone. He had a new family and, for him, it was a perfect fit.

Becoming part of a new family can be complicated. There are always Alpha dog rituals to work through. My parents were divorced when I was a teenager and when I moved in with my dad, his new wife and her two sons, we all had to learn to dance to a new tune.

Every family is distinct and each new person in the family adds a special dimension. Some families give the impression Norman Rockwell stepped into their living room and painted their portrait. Others seem to be living in an episode from "Halloween." However, most of our families actually fall somewhere in between those two extremes.

Did you know "family" was God's idea? Yep. He created it when He established the covenant of marriage. (Genesis 2:21-24) However, when Adam and Eve sinned, the family was the first thing to fall apart with Cain's murdering his brother Abel.

It's the God-given built-in need for family that stirs us with a longing to belong. According to some researchers, the need for identity, protection and belonging are high on the list of why many young people join gangs. And the overall deterioration of the family in our society unit hasn't helped.

In school, if we can't be a part of the "popular crowd," we rebel and join the anti-social clique (Isn't that an oxymoron?). We conform ourselves to fit in with our particular pack. We don the latest name-brand fashion or we dress like we barely survived a street fight. We put on the uniform and wear the colors all to fit into a "family."

As Christ-followers, we're part of a new family—the body of Christ. When we turn to God, He turns to us offering a spotless set of white clothes in exchange for our soiled suit of the past. Accepting Jesus as Lord of our lives brings us into the fold as sons and daughters of God. We have a new genetic code and a fresh look as we grow into the image of Christ. Our uniforms, while modest, vary but we do have our own "team color"—purple—for royalty.

Like Simon, we once faced life alone, disconnected and unsure of our future. We were helpless and ignorant until a resolute sponsor opened a door of opportunity for us and introduced us to a new family.

So, I'm inviting you to join my family. You'll fit right in. Hop in the car, but, please, don't throw up on my jeans!

***

Think about your family. Who are you? Whose are you?

For he chose us in him before the creation of the world to be holy and blameless in his sight. In love he predestined us for adoption to sonship through Jesus Christ, in accordance with his pleasure and will (Ephesians 1:4-5).

Chapter 2 – Stop Blowing that Whistle!

"When a dog runs at you, whistle for him."—
Henry David Thoreau

Ever heard of free-range chickens? They're our egg-laying friends who roam in the yard until sundown when they are brought home to roost in a chicken coop. In the country, farm dogs are often free-range too. Bailey and Simon certainly were.

Bailey loved galloping through the fields. She was taller and faster than Simon and often left him dragging his feet behind gasping for air. The two would spend the day exploring the wooded hills behind the house, returning exhausted in the evening. Bailey would come in the back door while we escorted Simon to his chain-link enclosure behind the garage where he could retire in his old, but roomy, doghouse.

If our roamers were late coming home, we would stand at the back door and blow a whistle. Neither Suki nor I learned the art of the finger-to-your-mouth ear-splitting country call, so we used a referee's whistle to call the dogs. The high-pitched

11

sound would pierce the valley like the blast of a train whistle in the distance. Before long we would see two blond tails high above the tall grass bouncing toward us.

One evening neither one of them came when we called, so out came the whistle. Three shorts blasts and a pause. Then, three more. Soon we heard the rustling of leaves as Bailey scampered around the garage—alone.

"Where's Simey?" I asked Bailey as if she could tell me. She glanced at me and trotted inside.

I strained to look for Simon in the dusky shadows. I blew three more blasts into the night air. Nothing stirred.

This was the first time Simon had ignored the whistle. We were worried. As darkness thickened, our fears grew. Every hour we went outside and blew the whistle but that rascal didn't come home. That night Suki retired to her room and I to mine, but we both couldn't sleep. *Where is Simon?*

My trips to the back door to call the dog only made the restless night longer. The next morning Simon was nowhere to be seen. We turned to Bailey for answers but she still wasn't talking. We blew the whistle again and again throughout the morning. *Where can he be?*

Later we had an appointment in town. In a few hours we returned, still worried about Simon.

Heading up the long driveway I saw movement in the pen behind the garage. "What's that?" I asked Suki.

We looked more closely as we pulled up. Simon's blond head was bouncing up and down like a Yo-Yo as he tried to bound over the chain-link fence. The dog was in his pen!

What had happened?

Using our combined brainpower we figured that instead of coming to the back door the night before, he had gone straight to bed. The gate had closed behind him, and he was trapped.

I imagined him lying in his doghouse the night before wondering, *What are they doing? I'm dog-tired and can't even get a good catnap. Stop blowing the whistle!*

When we opened the gate, he leapt into the yard, spun around and wiggled a joyful "hello." Then he raced off to find Bailey.

Sometimes we blow our own whistle for God to rescue us over and over, without realizing God has already answered our prayer. *Stop blowing that whistle!*

Suki and I often pray with people who want God to restore their lives with no effort on their part. While God is all-powerful and could instantly rescue them, He usually won't. He's more concerned with the long-term goal of character building than making our problems disappear. His solution is often within our reach; however, in my experience, God also expects something from us. Let me illustrate.

A woman may want God to "fix" her marriage—in other words, her husband. After listening to the list of his offenses, Suki and I point her to 1 Corinthians 13: "(Love) keeps no record of wrongs." Marriage scorecards are as helpful as a two-legged stool. However, every time she forgives her husband, she entrusts her marriage to God. He will work on the husband's heart, but often the "fix" will be in her first.

God will do His part if we will do ours. *Stop blowing that whistle!*

In Israel's on-again, off-again relationship with God He cleared a path for them to emerge from 400 years of slavery in Egypt. He answered their whistle by sending Moses.

You know the story. God parted the Red Sea and led them to the border of Canaan. He told Moses to send 12 spies into the territory and bring back a report about the land He promised them. When they returned, all said the land was bountiful. But only two of the spies, Joshua and Caleb, were ready to take their inheritance. The other ten were afraid. (Numbers 12:33)

God had fulfilled His promise, but it wasn't what they were expecting. Instead of taking the land, they kept blowing their whistle. So God let them wander 40 more years.

In the New Testament, the Israelites still didn't get it. God had promised to send a Savior, a

14

Messiah, and the Pharisees were waiting for Him. They were whistling to God and looking for His Chosen One to appear, when all the time Jesus was standing right in front of them.

I don't want to miss Jesus. How about you? Instead of blowing the whistle and asking God to step in to change my situation, I'm trying to see where He is in my circumstances. He's always there and He has a solution.

Sometimes He wants me to step into the battle and fight, while other times He expects me to back up and let Him do the fighting. Often He asks me to pray and occasionally He wants me to give. Whatever the situation, He's already there.

Simon has become such a homebody we rarely use the whistle anymore. He stays close enough to hear me when I call his name. That's how I want my relationship with God to be.

I don't want to waste time whistling only to discover He's been there all along.

***

Are you whistling for God to intervene in your life? Has He been there all along?

And after the fire came a gentle whisper. When Elijah heard it, he pulled his cloak over his face and went out and stood at the mouth of the cave. Then a voice said to him, "What are you doing here, Elijah?" (1 Kings 19:12-13).

Chapter 3 – The Car

"Dogs are wise. They crawl away into a quiet corner and lick their wounds and do not rejoin the world until they are whole once more." —Agatha Christie

"Simon's been hit!"

I sprang out of bed and threw on some clothes as I raced for the front door. Panic was strangling the breath out of me.

Suki charged through the yard toward Simon who was howling as only a wounded dog can. Although his right hind leg was pulled tight to his body, the lower part of his leg dangled lifelessly. The three of us met at the edge of the field where Simon collapsed on his side, whimpering. He had run the length of a football field on three legs to get to us.

I cradled his head and tried to keep him calm while Suki sprinted for the truck. He didn't resist when we slipped a towel under him and used it as a stretcher to lift him onto the back seat. I crawled

17

in after him. There was no blood but his back leg was broken. So was my heart.

"Simon was crossing the road when the car hit him," Suki's voice trembled as she drove to the animal clinic. "The car never stopped. It didn't even slow down!"

Simey looked up at me with pleading eyes as if to say, "Please fix it." He was calmer now, but his heart was still racing. I called Dr. Amy, his veterinarian, while Suki drove.

She was ready for us when we arrived. Her assistants met us at the door. We swept past the waiting room in a blur as Dr. Amy took our boy in for X-rays. With our adrenalin pumping, Suki and I prayed and paced the floor like hamsters running on a wheel.

Dr. Amy had been our vet ever since we had moved to town. Her compassion for our pets and her amiable personality made the trip to the doctor an easy one for Bailey and Simon and for Suki and me. She loves her four-legged patients and has a natural ability to put them at ease.

The door opened. Dr. Amy's face was grim. We braced ourselves for bad news.

"Well, Ladies," she sighed as she hung the X-rays on the light board on the wall. "It's not good." She pointed to the image of Simon's leg. "The bone is broken in two places—here and here." We could easily see the fractures. A two-inch section of his bone had been completely severed. "This part of the bone will die if we can't restore the blood

18

flow. It must be reattached. It's a complicated surgery and he could lose his leg."

Suki and I were stunned as we looked down at our suffering little one still panting on the cart.

"I can amputate his leg," Dr. Amy said. "He'll be able to get around just fine on three legs." I clenched my jaw against the rising tears. "Or you could take him to a specialist," she suggested. "There's an excellent doctor in Nashville who might be able to repair the damage, but it will be expensive."

Thoughts blew through my mind like a shotgun blast. *He's not a horse. We can't simply put him down. He's only nine months old! We've got to try.*

We decided to take him to Nashville. Dr. Amy handed us Simon's X-rays and said she would call the specialist to let him know we were coming.

Once again I sat in the backseat talking to Simey and stroking his face to keep him calm. He lay quietly, afraid to move, his eyes still pleading. We made the hour-long drive to Music City in 45 minutes.

Assistants met us with a stretcher and wheeled Simon through the waiting room lined with autographed photos from country music legends. The pictures had inscriptions like, "Thanks for your wonderful care of Fi Fi!"

Suki and I glanced at one another. I could hear the money draining from our bank accounts like coins flowing from a slot machine—paying out to someone else!

The doctor came in and immediately put a muzzle over Simon's mouth. Our pup was confused and so were we. "Why are you doing that? He won't bite," I said.

"No matter how gentle a dog is, if he's in pain he could snap at you," he said as he turned to look at the X-rays.

"This floating bone is the problem," the specialist said. "Without a blood supply it will die." His words were identical to Dr. Amy's.

He showed us a thin metal plate. "This will hold his leg in place until it heals, but we can't be sure the bone will grow back together. Only time will tell. We'll prep him for surgery and you can pick him up in two days."

One ten-inch-long steel plate, 26 screws and $2500 later we brought home a scarred and groggy Simon. He now donned the latest-style plastic megaphone-shaped Elizabethan collar to keep him from licking the incision. The doctor had these parting instructions: "Keep him inside for six weeks."

"But he's an outside dog." Now it was my turn to whine.

"Then keep him in a pen. The plate is not designed to be weight-bearing. It will keep his leg stationary until the bone knits together again, but he can't take more than 10,000 steps on that leg for the next six weeks or it won't heal properly."

The specialist added, "And keep the Elizabethan collar on him until the incision heals."

Simon lived in his pen for a month and a half. The only exceptions were his twice-daily leash-led bathroom breaks to the field a few feet away and short visits with our friends who signed his collar like high school kids autographing a football hero's cast.

Six weeks later Simon received a clean bill of health. New X-rays showed the bones had fused beautifully and our four-legged furball was free to sprint around the yard untethered. We celebrated as Simon galloped in the field with Bailey. Except for the S-shaped scar down his right thigh, you would never know his leg had been broken. He was "good as new."

We've all been hit by cars as we amble down life's road: a fractured friendship, a bone-jarring dismissal at work, a drive-by bully, a broken marriage, a visit to the doctor who says, "I can't fix this." Some situations seem impossible and we don't know how we will survive. May I suggest survival isn't the primary issue? Coping with the problem is.

In my own past, when I hit a wall (or the wall hit me) I alternately turned to drugs, sex or alcohol. I wanted to escape the harsh reality in front of me as I tried to find a little comfort— something to dull the pain. The solutions I turned to, however, only worked until the "high" wore off.

At my wit's end, I finally broke down and prayed, "God, if You are real, I need to know."

That was all He needed. Lightning didn't strike. The sky didn't explode with the brilliance of a new sun. The air didn't vibrate with gold dust swirling around my head. However, God answered my prayer and something in me changed forever, and I knew it.

The change wasn't external. It was internal. All the turmoil inside me scattered like leaves in the wind and a peace settled over me. At that moment I knew God was real and I realized I had been looking for "real" all my life.

The reality of God became the solution to my problems. Now, when a car comes barreling toward me, like anyone with half a brain, I get out of the way. If, however, I can't dodge the Dodge and I end up with something broken; I have a Specialist, Who, one way or another, can make everything right again.

Simon has never limped or favored his broken leg—even in damp weather. And, frankly, I'm not sure he even remembers being hit by a car. As far as he's concerned, if he can limp his way to us, everything's fixable.

Whatever pain you're in, if you can limp your way to God, you'll always hear Him say, "I can fix this."

***

Are you in a circumstance that seems unfixable? How can you handle it?

Do not be anxious about anything, but in every situation, by prayer and petition, with thanksgiving, present your requests to God. And the peace of God, which transcends all understanding, will guard your hearts and your minds in Christ Jesus (Philippians 4:6-7).

Chapter 4 – Let it Snow, Let it Snow, Let it Snow

"Happiness is a warm puppy."—Charles M. Schulz

"Snow flurries are expected and temperatures will drop well below zero tonight," warned the TV weatherman. In Tennessee, that's code for "Hightail it to the grocery store and buy all the milk, bread and toilet paper you can carry." All it takes is the rumor of snow to persuade us to close our schools, stay home from work and stock up on the necessities of life! We pull out the blankets, check the batteries in the flashlights, locate every candle in the house, pop the popcorn, heat up the cocoa, put on our favorite movie and make plans to settle in for a week.

Okay. Don't raise your eyebrow at me simply because you're a seasoned snow-tired, chain totin', four-wheeling driver living north of the Mason Dixon line.

A couple of inches of snow is an event around here. We build 12-inch-tall snowmen (because that's all the snow we can find) and post dozens of Facebook photos of decks looking like they've been dusted with confectioners' sugar. After all, the world needs to see the inconvenient beauty of being trapped in an icy Winter Wonderland in Tennessee.

We gave all our attention to the man in front of the map of the Southeast as he continued his winter storm advisory. "Don't leave your pets outside tonight. Make sure they have a warm place to stay."

Suki looked at me. "You'll have to bring Simon in." (After all, he's "my dog.")

An inch of icy slush was already on the ground so I donned my insulated jacket with a hood, wrapped a scarf around my neck and crammed my feet into heavy boots. Fat flakes fell as I slogged the 30-yard hike from the house to the dog pen where Simon lived. He was curled up sleeping in his doghouse.

He looked up at me as if to say, "What are you doing out in this weather?"

"Come on, Simon. We're going in the house."

He gave his head a shake as if to say, "Am I hearing this right?" I repeated myself.

That was all he needed. It was as if he'd been waiting to hear those words all his life. Scrambling out of his doghouse, he flew past me racing to the back door. He was waiting for me with his tail wagging as I made my way through the "blizzard" back to the house.

Simon continued his wiggle as I wiped his muddy feet. I opened the door and he bounded in. After a brief "hello," he headed for Bailey's food bowl. He gobbled down her leftovers then promptly made himself at home on her pillow by the fire, in a doggy version of "Goldilocks and the Three Bears." With one final sigh he settled in with a full belly and a warm soft bed. As the story goes, "It was just right."

Simon never slept in his pen again. In one short night our pup had been permanently relocated from an outside dog to an inside dog.

As Christ-followers we've been relocated, too. We once lived on the outside, in the cold, separated from the family. We compensated by curling up in a self-absorbed ball, consoling ourselves while we waited for an open door and an invitation. We could see the warmth, comfort and fellowship inside the Master's house, but we didn't know how to get in. We didn't have permission. We needed someone to unlock the door and let us out of our pen.

That Someone is Jesus. He has the door open wide and the invitation in His hand. Yet some of us don't want to come out of our cramped doghouses. We curl up on a hard, cold wooden floor and try to convince ourselves we're comfortable. We make excuses saying, "The big house isn't for me," and we settle.

We live below the Kingdom standard and assert this is where we're supposed to be. We've become so accustomed to living in the doghouse; we no longer notice the hard floor or the icy wind. Perhaps we believe we don't deserve anything better.

Another reason we stay in the pen is we don't want to step into the chilly breeze of humility. It takes courage to step out of our "comfort zone," even if only for a moment. We tell ourselves we'll make it through the night if we can curl up and turn inward. The only problem is, all the while we're freezing to death.

Even though Simon was part of the family, when he was in the pen, he was missing out on all the blessings that come from family fellowship. Sometimes we miss out on the blessings of the Kingdom too. We may say our prayers and go to church, but the fullness of the Kingdom hasn't yet come into our lives. We've been accepted into the family, but we haven't come into the house.

I once heard a pastor say, "I spend my life barely making ends meet." I was sad for him. We know we are not to spend our lives storing up worldly possessions. Most of our homes are stuffed with too much stuff already. But neither are we to preach the twisted notion that poverty is a sure sign of holiness.

While Jesus never owned a home, He never lived in lack. As a friend of mine used to say, "He had a lack of lack." And that's what living in the Kingdom looks like. Jesus wants us to be blessed and prosperous so we can bless others. God even tells us to test Him in this. If we're faithful to give one-tenth of our resources to God, He promises to open His storehouses of blessings on us.[1]

If you haven't left the pen yet, Jesus is holding the open door for you too.

Come on in. It's too chilly to stay outside and I think you'll find, "It's just right."

***

Are you still resisting Jesus' open door? Why don't you accept His invitation for more?

The Lord does not let the righteous go hungry, but he thwarts the craving of the wicked (Proverbs 10:3).

---

[1] Malachi 3:10.

Chapter 5 – A New Me

"Why does watching a dog be a dog fill one with happiness?" —*Jonathan Safran Foer*

Simon and Bailey were as different as night and day. When we met Bailey, she was tethered on a short chain at the end of an open shed. Exposed electrical wires were within gnawing distance of her empty food bowl. She had often missed a meal in her two-year-old life because her owners had forgotten to feed her.

Like a neglected piece of equipment, she was invisible to her owners who, truthfully, didn't want her. Bailey's advocate and our rescue representative, Janie, told us the family had once left for a week-long vacation without putting out food for her. They let her loose, hoping she would wander off.

When we "rescued" her, she was skittish and withdrawn. At first, we had to keep her on a leash because she didn't know where home was and she trusted no one. Bailey didn't understand she had been adopted into a new family who would love her and take care of her. Bailey saw herself as a neglected piece of property. In her mind she had no privileges. She had a slave mentality.

Simon was also a rescue dog, but was only about 9-months-old when he came to live with us. Although he hadn't suffered like Bailey, he had been abandoned and was already learning to survive on his own. He had developed an orphan mentality.

When it was dinnertime, timid Bailey always let Simon gobble down his fill before she approached her bowl. Simon was the pushy Alpha pup. Their behavior reflected who they believed they were—whether or not it was true.

If Bailey had a toy, Simon wanted it—even though he didn't play with toys. If Bailey got attention, Simon wanted more. The only time Bailey would stand her ground was when it came to Suki. She knew she was Suki's almond-eyed girl and wouldn't let Simon near her.

Whether slave or orphan, both of our adopted pups needed a major mind modification. We knew it would take time, and lots of love.

As Christ-followers, we gladly accept the salvation of the cross, yet we often carry around an old suitcase filled with lies about who we are. The salvation is instant; changing the way we think takes time. Jesus died on the cross so we could be transformed from slaves and orphans to sons and daughters. Let's dig through our baggage and throw out those smelly socks stuffed in the corner.

In Romans 8:15 Paul says, "The Spirit you received does not make you slaves, so that you live in fear again; rather, the Spirit you received brought about your adoption to sonship." In John 15:15 Jesus says, "I no longer call you servants, because a servant does not know his master's business. Instead, I have called you friends ..." Servants and slaves do what they're told. They're never included in the family's fellowship and they're not allowed to sit at the table or lounge on the furniture.

We're not slaves, nor are we orphans (unloved and unwelcome). We don't have to beg for God's favor or His left-overs. We already have access to the best He has to offer. He's laid out a banquet table before us and pulled out a chair. Isn't it time we took a seat at the table and stopped sniffing the floor underneath for crumbs. We're children of God—loved and accepted and part of the family.

Everything in the Kingdom (God's house) is available to us. Metaphorically, we can reach into Heaven and pull it down to earth. Jesus said so in His prayer recorded in Matthew 6: "Your kingdom come, your will be done, on earth as it is in heaven." Our prayers open Heaven's doors so we can enter.

We have a seat at the table. Like President Kennedy's son, John-John, crawling under his dad's desk in the Oval Office while decisions of national importance are being made above, we have access to our Father anywhere and anytime. That's what being a son or daughter means.

No matter how long we've been a Christ-follower, our self-talk regularly needs adjusting. Old ideas and old self-images will always try to creep in. Like tying a string around our finger, reading God's Word awakens us to who we are and Whose we are. Both the Old and New Testaments begin with family trees—God's reminder we are part of a family.

Isn't it time to let go of our old baggage? After all God has given us new matching luggage, filled with His promises. He's ready to bring out our royal robe, slip a ring on our finger (alongside that string), lay out the banquet, throw us a party and give us a closet full of shoes (that's for us daughters). The celebration has begun. Let's step forward to take our inheritance.

It took a long time and a lot of love to "retrain" Bailey's and Simon's way of thinking.

Bailey eventually learned we were safe. She began to trust us, which meant she no longer needed a leash. Simon accepted his new situation more quickly (perhaps because he was younger). They both were free to come and go, but after a day's adventures they always came home to the family where they belonged.

Over time Bailey accepted some things as hers. She had her own pillow, and a crate with an open door, which we draped with a towel. It was her own little "house." She had her own toys, too.

She loved squeaky tennis balls and hid them everywhere. She would chew them until the squeakers broke and then, continue gnawing on them to hear them pop—for hours!

Simon stopped being jealous and soon even ignored her toys. He also stopped gobbling up all the food. He eventually learned he would always have enough, so he began eating more like a cat—only when he was hungry. Now he leaves food behind for between-meal snacks.

As Christ-followers you and I are children of the King. We have access to everything He has. It's all laid out before us. The table is always set and it's always brimming over with delightful treats.

All we have to do is take our seat.

***

Can you identify with either the slave or orphan mentality? What lies do you need to renounce to accept that you're a child of God?

So you are no longer a slave, but God's child; and since you are his child, God has made you also an heir (Galatians 4:7).

Chapter 6 – The Chicken

"In a dog-eat-dog world, it is the dogmatic domain of dog lovers to offer dogdom a dog's chance to rise above the dog days for a doggone good time."—AKC Gazette, August, 1991

Simon followed Bailey everywhere. She would lead him on high adventures playing hide and seek in the woods or splashing through the stream in a game of tag. There were animal tracks to follow, scents to uncover, races to run and neighbors to meet—both two-legged and four-legged. These two daredevils explored hills, fields, creeks and ponds. And when the day was done, with tongues hanging out the sides of their mouths, they would drag their tired bodies home where supper and warm beds were waiting.

One afternoon after a day of exploring parts unknown, Bailey came trotting up the driveway with something large and black in her mouth. Simon was jogging alongside her. They looked like excited children bringing home straight-A report cards.

As our tail-wagging friends drew closer, Suki and I saw the black thing in Bailey's mouth was a chicken!

Oh no, I thought. *Bailey murdered a chicken!* That's a serious crime in farming communities. Country dogs who kill farm animals usually end up permanently behind the bars of a dog pen or on Wanted Dead or Alive posters secretly circulated among underground bounty-hunters throughout the county.

The dogs stopped at the edge of the yard, and Bailey put down her limp wet treasure. She smiled at us, waiting for our praise. Instead, we met her with panic as we realized we would have to greet our neighbor with bad news.

A farmer down the road raised chickens on his small farm. We hadn't met our neighbors yet, but knocking on their door with a dead chicken in our hands didn't seem to be the best way to start a friendship.

Time froze.

The four of us looked at one another in confusion. Then to our surprise the chicken clucked, stood up, ruffled her feathers and indignantly strutted away! Bailey circled around the bird to pick her up again. We stared at her in amazement. Bailey had carried a fresh take-out chicken dinner in her mouth for a quarter of a mile without so much as a nibble.

The dogs didn't want to eat the bird—they wanted to play with her!

Like hitting the play button on a paused DVR, Suki and I leapt into action grabbing for the dogs. I wrestled with Simon while Suki grabbed Bailey by the collar. Quickly, we ushered our poultry predators into the house. The chicken was safe— for the moment!

With the dogs out of our way we returned to the yard to capture the offended hen, hoping to return the little clucker to her home. Have you ever tried to grab a traumatized chicken? With arms and legs windmilling the two of us chased that bird left and right around the yard. When we zigged, she zagged.

We tried to corner her in the bushes only to have her scoot through our legs at the last minute. I never realized how fast those clucking critters could move. When we ran out of breath, we did our best to make friends and lure her into our grasp. The silly bird didn't trust us. Who could blame her? Finally, we tried to herd her down the road toward her home but she kept doubling back behind us. Every attempt failed.

Exhausted, we collapsed on the front porch. The crazy chicken, having enjoyed the exercise, settled down to scratching around the yard. Like movie-goers at a matinee, Simon and Bailey watched the show from the front window.

We kept the dogs in the house the rest of the day, hoping the chicken would figure out how to go home; however, as the day wore on we became less and less hopeful. Evidently, this feathered foreigner liked playing in our yard.

The next morning there was no sign of the chicken. "She probably found her way home in the night," Suki said as we let the dogs out. However, in only a few minutes we discovered the chicken hadn't gone home after all. Our happy hunters had sniffed out her location under a bush by the pond. They were playing with her, pawing at her, cornering her and nudging her. The two mutts were having great fun.

By the time we got down to the pond again to rescue the chicken, she was lying on the ground lifeless. This time she really was dead. The dogs were looking at her as if they couldn't figure out why she stopped playing with them. There wasn't a mark on the bird. They hadn't bitten her. They simply couldn't resist the temptation and they "played" her to death.

As we gathered up the feathered remains, the dogs bounded off into the woods headed for a new adventure. It was time to speak with the farmer down the road.

With dread we knocked on our neighbor's door. We introduced ourselves and explained what happened.

"She probably got out through the hole in the fence," the gracious farmer admitted. "Don't worry about it. She was only a chicken. These things happen." He accepted our apologies. We paid him for his loss and returned home, grateful for his understanding.

Have you ever played with something that led to harm? I have. How many times have we used these lines: "What could it hurt?" "Everyone else was doing it." "It was only a game." "I wasn't serious." "I didn't start it," "It wasn't my idea," "I didn't mean for anything bad to happen."

We barely stick our toes in the water and in no time at all we're being sucked under like getting caught in an eddy. That's the nature of sin—it looks innocent at first. It starts small; then it pulls us in until we're caught. We think we can control it, and we do for a while. But eventually it ends up controlling us.

"The game" begins with a hole in the fence— an opportunity.

When I was in college, I found an unopened pack of cigarettes on a bench outside the cafeteria and I took it back to the dorm. *What harm can it do to try it?* My roommate and I both decided to try smoking—for fun. We rationalized, "Everyone else is doing it."

We lit up and thought we looked cool smoking. When the pack was empty, I bought another—to keep up the image. "It's not serious."

I thought I could control it, but soon it was controlling me. I was hooked.

Then the excuses came. "I didn't start it." Someone left that first pack on a bench. "It wasn't my idea." "I didn't mean for anything bad to happen." "I was only playing."

Even though we may not have "started it," we're as guilty as the one who did. Somewhere along the line we made a choice to keep going.

After ten years I was smoking four packs a day. I was addicted. Then my mom, who was also a smoker, died of lung cancer. The next month, on Great American Smoke-Out Day, I smoked my last cigarette.

We can make all the excuses we want, but ultimately the choice is ours. I was the one who took the cigarettes back to my room. No one held a gun to my head and forced me to smoke them. I made up my mind to buy another pack. Temptation presented itself and I invited it in. Instead of taking charge of my life, I gave up control to an enemy who doesn't play games. He follows up on every temptation leaving us to cope with the consequences.

God has given us all good boundaries. However, in our rebellious nature, we're often found searching for the hole in the fence. When we find it we can push our way through or stay inside in the security of His protection. He will not stop us even when our choices are harmful.

Managing our lives is much easier if we learn to resist the temptation when it comes.

After all, who wants a dead chicken on their back porch?

***

Have you been sucked into something thinking it's harmless? What are some ways to resist temptation when it comes?

No temptation has overtaken you except what is common to mankind. And God is faithful; he will not let you be tempted beyond what you can bear. But when you are tempted, he will also provide a way out so that you can endure it (1 Corinthians 10:13).

Chapter 7 – I Could Kill That Dog!

"Dogs are great. Bad dogs, if you can really call them that, are perhaps the greatest of them all." — *John Grogan*

Simon was barking when we got home from church. He recognized the car and was overjoyed to see us—for good reason. It had rained all night so the ground in his pen was soaked and muddy. Suki opened the door of the six-foot-tall fenced enclosure and Simon eagerly pounced. He jumped up on his hind feet and slapped his front paws on Suki's shoulders in a frenzied puppy greeting.

I stuffed the chuckle in my throat when I saw Suki's face. Her nice Sunday clothes were splattered with mud and she was madder than a mosquito in a mannequin factory. "I could kill that dog!" She hollered as I retreated into the house.

The mud came out of her clothes, but the welcome home pouncing continued. We tried everything to curb Simon's enthusiastic greetings. We would command him to sit. (Have you ever seen a dog sit, but not sit?) In his excitement he

45

would take the sitting pose, but his muscles would be coiled and ready for the leap. Before we could say, "Good boy," he was already back on all fours.

We tried hiding behind the gate when we swung it open, but that darn dog would dart around behind the door with us. We even tried jumping in the pen while he bounded out, but that simply delayed the inevitable. Simon would wait till we came out, then pounce.

Eventually, Suki refused to open Simon's pen—after all, he was "my dog." I gave up trying to outwit him so I kept a set of "letting-Simon-out-of-the-pen clothes" in the utility room. As much as I tried to train him otherwise, he was still a bouncing, pouncing puppy. I hoped he would grow out of it, but that could take years, and I wasn't willing to wait.

Simon greeted company with the same enthusiasm he had for us, but it wasn't acceptable for him to jump on our guests. Our solution? The shock collar.

Using shock collars is one way dog owners train their pets. While they could be called a "lazy man's dog school," we were at our wit's end so we tried it. It didn't work.

Simon didn't get it. He didn't associate the pain from the small electronic shock with the correction. And we didn't like the idea of using something that hurt him. The shock collar went into the drawer.

Then we found another training device we did like. It was a remote control gadget that emitted sound waves only the dog could hear. The sound to him must have been shrill and irritating. When Simon jumped, we would point the remote control at him, say, "Sit," and push the button. He learned to sit, not jump, when company came to the door. Soon he was so attuned to the gizmo that if we couldn't find it, we picked up the TV remote or pointed our phones at him and he would sit. Within a few weeks we didn't need the device at all. Problem solved!

We all have areas in our lives where our enthusiasm overrides our discipline. May I step on your toes a bit? Eating, shopping, television, computer games, smoking and social media are some of the places where we need our own version of a shock collar. How about an extra helping of cake? Maybe only half a piece. Zing! I love those shoes. I'll take two pairs. They're on sale! Zip!

In his letter to the Galatians Paul says self-control is one of the fruits of the Spirit—and, believe me, when I'm ready to jump only the Holy Spirit can cause me to put the brakes on. Does it surprise anyone that discipline is not a popular sermon topic? The truth is, we don't want any restraints—at least, I don't. I want to indulge myself without any of the consequences. After all, I've had a hard day sitting at the computer putting words together. Surely, I've earned a shopping spree—to the grocery store!

Living without self-control can be damaging, if not disastrous. Undisciplined behavior can shatter marriages, bring on debt, isolate family members, cause health issues, wreck communication and ruin our self-image. Interestingly, if we decide to fix the problem on our own, we usually make it worse.

In our self-determination to repair the damage we can swing in the opposite direction like a pendulum on a grandfather clock. We over-exercise or go on crazy diets; we become miserly or borrow unwisely; we stuff our emotions or refuse to talk about them.

Fixing our self-discipline issues our way usually ends up with us replacing one idol with another. In 1969 singer Frank Sinatra released a song, "My Way,"[2] that became a theme for him. The climactic last line asserts, "I did it my way." The song implies that if we are strong enough, or tough enough, or stubborn enough we don't need help or advice. But that's not true. The only kind of self-control that works comes from the Holy Spirit. He's the One Who gives us the strength to overcome.

As we learn to say, "No" to ourselves we begin to develop better behavior patterns. Scripture calls it "dying to our flesh." When we lay down our selfish desires, we make room in our hearts for God's nature to move in. In that way we are being

---

[2] Paul Anka,"My Way," (Reprise Records, 1969).

changed from "glory to glory" as God gently molds us into the image of Christ.

Spiritual growth is simply the process of getting better at responding to the Holy Spirit's nudges. I don't know about you, but I want to be quick to forgive, quick to repent and quick to respond to what the Holy Spirit says.

Simon's a better pet since he's learned to behave. He welcomes company properly—without jumping. Now he usually barks a "hello," wags his tail and escorts our visitors to the front door.

Of course, I do have room for an extra pair of shoes in my closet.

Zap!

***

Do you have self-control issues in your life? Are you willing to ask the Holy Spirit for help?

For the grace of God has appeared that offers salvation to all people. It teaches us to say "No" to ungodliness and worldly passions, and to live self-controlled, upright and godly lives in this present age (Titus 2:11-12).

Chapter 8 – What's INSIDE the Box

"You know, a dog can snap you out of any kind of bad mood that you're in faster than you can think of."—Jill Abramson

With his tail wagging and a smile on his lips, Simon greets the UPS deliveryman like they're old friends. When the truck pulls up in the driveway, our furry greeter is quick to hop on board and sniff the parcels. He loves boxes.

When we bring the package into the house, Simon is only mildly curious until we slit through the tape and pull back the flaps. When the carton is emptied, it's fair game for an inquisitive pooch who thinks every cardboard box is his newest toy.

We discovered his love of cardboard during Simon's first Christmas with us. We had wrapped toys for him and Bailey and put them under the tree. On the Big Day we gave each of them their presents, only to find Simon snubbed his squeaky toy for a second helping of the wrapping. And when his carton was thoroughly chewed, he left his mushy mess to gnaw on Bailey's empty box, not the toy.

Gifts and even food go unnoticed as Simon devotes all his energy to the cardboard. Holding the box in his paws, he bites at the corners until a piece pulls away. He chews it a bit, then he spits it out and starts the process all over again until the box is destroyed.

I've learned the hard way to examine what I bring home from the store as soon as I take it out of the package in case it must be returned. Otherwise the box it came in will end up in soggy spit-out pieces on the floor. I think it's the process of pulling and tearing that Simon loves. The cardboard itself has no appetizing or aesthetic appeal so he spits it out.

Do you realize we can be so distasteful to God He will spit us out? There's a sobering passage in the book of Revelation written by the apostle John. While imprisoned on the Isle of Patmos off the coast of Greece, he had a vision in which Jesus appeared with a message to seven churches in Asia. (Revelation 1:19)

In His message to the church in Laodicea Jesus gives this warning: "I know your deeds, that you are neither cold nor hot. I wish you were either one or the other! So, because you are lukewarm—neither hot nor cold—I am about to spit you out of my mouth."

Laodicea had many resources, but water wasn't one of them. A system of aqueducts brought mineral water from hot springs in Baspinar six miles away, but by the time it arrived in the city it was lukewarm. Because it was unsuitable for drinking, a second system of aqueducts was built to bring cold water from the Lycos river at Colosse. Again, because of the distance of the pipeline, the water arrived lukewarm.

Laodicea had neither hot nor cold water and scholars believe Jesus was referring to this problem when He addressed the church. To all outward appearances Laodicea had everything. It was one of the wealthiest cities in the ancient world and the church reflected that prosperity. By all accounts the church was thriving.

I imagine the Laodicean church had an impressive building where they held filled-to-capacity coliseum conferences with talented toga-clad musicians leading worship. They probably had a dynamic preacher, interactive Sunday school classes and numerous charitable institutions. However, their deeds lacked the love, joy or fire that comes from a relationship with the Spirit of the Living God. When Jesus looked at the church, He saw beyond the brightly decorated facade into the tepid, stagnant recesses of the heart.

He sees through us, too. Do we dress up and go through a weekly religious routine because "that's what we're supposed to do?" Do we put on a smile for an hour only to get in the car and fight about where we're going to eat for lunch? Do we put Jesus in a box at noon to watch the ball game and leave Him there until the next Sunday morning? Believe me, Jesus sees it and He has a name for it—hypocrisy.

It's the same word He used when talking about the religious leaders of His day. He called them hypocrites because they gave an outward show of their piety, when they had no love, joy or fire for God in their hearts. He said they were whitewashed tombs—clean and white on the outside, yet dead on the inside.

Jesus cares more about who we are on the inside than what we do or how we look on the outside. Lukewarm living is lifeless living. It's scraping by, living in a daze, wasting away, shuffling through our days without a goal. Our purpose and potential get lost in the murky, sluggish water of apathy.

But wait! There's a remedy. Jesus says, "Look inside your heart." If you're a Christ-follower, ask God to awaken His Spirit living inside you. If you're not, ask God to breathe life into your heart. That's right; all we have to do is ask God. It's that simple.

No matter where you stand, I promise if you ask Him, God will come. When He does, you'll feel like someone has turned on both taps of the faucet—hot and cold. You'll feel the cool refreshing breath of the Holy Spirit washing away your depression and bringing new life and hope. AND you'll discover a new spark beginning to burn inside your heart. As it spreads like a flame on the corner of a newspaper, it will grow into a fire that can't be contained. So say goodbye to lukewarm.

Stop chewing the soggy cardboard box and receive the gift inside. I guarantee there's absolutely nothing lukewarm about this Gift!

***

Are you hot or cold or lukewarm? How can you "turn up the heat" on your faith?

I know your deeds, that you are neither cold nor hot. I wish you were either one or the other! So, because you are lukewarm—neither hot nor cold—I am about to spit you out of my mouth (Revelation 3:15-16).

Chapter 9 – Where's Bailey?

"God will prepare everything for our perfect happiness in heaven, and if it takes my dog being there, I believe he'll be there."—Billy Graham

It had been a dry summer. Creeks and ponds were waterless leaving rotten leaves and swampy areas exposed. For a couple of four-legged explorers the drought brought altogether different adventures and smells. Things previously hidden became new discoveries keeping Bailey out until the shadows grew long and the growling in her stomach brought her home. They were lighthearted, carefree days for an inquisitive roamer.

Simon, on the other hand, usually stayed closer to home. Either the drawn-out days of wandering tired him out faster than Bailey, or he simply wasn't as interested in sniffing under *every* log in the woods.

Toward the end of the summer we had to go out of town for a few days. We left the dogs with a house sitter and told her not to worry if the dogs were gone all day. After all, they were the Indiana Joneses of the neighborhood—just as long as they didn't bring home a chicken!

When we returned home, Simon, as usual, greeted us halfway down the drive with a wagging tail and joyous barks. He trotted alongside the car like a secret service agent guarding the presidential motorcade. Bailey, as usual, was nowhere to be seen. When she did come home, she seemed to be pouting, which she often did when we were gone longer than she deemed appropriate.

The next day she was still punishing us. She was stand-offish and would retreat to the shade of the deck or the bushes around the house. We weren't concerned until that evening when she started wheezing, sucking in air like she couldn't get her breath.

"We should take her to the vet," Suki suggested.

The next day we put Simon in his pen and piled Bailey into the truck. Dr. Amy listened to her chest and said. "We need some X-rays."

We waited.

Dr. Amy had a grim expression on her face as she entered the room and attached the film of Bailey's lungs to the lighted panel on the wall.

"This area that looks like snow in her lungs is blastomycosis," she explained. "It's an infection caused by a fungus called Blastomyces found in moist soil and decomposing leaves. The microscopic spores are breathed in and begin to

58

multiply. You can see her lungs are almost completely covered which is why she's struggling to breathe."

Suki and I looked down at our exhausted little girl resting on the cool floor.

"We can prescribe some medicine that might help," Dr. Amy suggested, "but it's expensive and the fungus is pretty far advanced."

"We'll do whatever it takes," Suki said.

"It must be taken daily," Dr. Amy instructed us as she wrote out a prescription. "You'll have to get this filled at a pharmacy."

"We're heading to West Virginia next week to spend Thanksgiving with family," Suki said. "Should we cancel our trip?"

"No. Bring her here. We'll take care of her. We'll spend time with her every day so she won't be lonely and we'll make sure she gets her medication."

Bailey stayed home that week. She wasn't interested in roaming anymore. When she felt like going outside, she would crawl under the back deck and lie down in the cool darkness. Knowing something was wrong, Simon stayed close, sitting beside her in the flowerbed or wherever she went. He didn't even mind when we gave her yummy canned dog food instead of the usual dried kibbles.

The next week, with sad hearts, we packed the car and took Simon to the kennel—alone. Then we dropped Bailey off at Dr. Amy's.

"We'll take good care of her," Dr. Amy assured us. With my throat closed I simply nodded as we gave Bailey a goodbye hug.

The six-hour drive was mostly quiet. Sadness settled over us as we each inwardly coped with Bailey's condition. We tried to focus on the coming family gathering, but concern for Bailey was always gnawing at the edge of our thoughts.

Arriving that evening we told the family about Bailey. Grief was already trying to claw its way to the surface, but we kept pushing it down—determined to concentrate on the holiday.

The next morning, however, our hopes plunged when my phone showed three missed calls from the vet. "This is not going to be good," I said to Suki as I hit redial.

Dr. Amy answered. "I'm so sorry," she began. We knew the rest. "When we came in this morning Bailey had passed away in the night." The grief we had been resisting finally broke the surface. Tears spilled down our cheeks, squeezed out by the tightness in our chests. It was Thanksgiving Day and our beloved Bailey-Girl was gone.

Over the next several hours, the food was prepared, the table set and the prayers were said, but Suki and I were on automatic pilot. We put on brave faces, but wanted to retreat and lick our wounds. Family was supportive and sympathetic, but the day was long.

How do you give thanks when your heart is crushed? Thankfulness had slipped to the bottom of the pile of our emotions. Like dancing at a funeral, the words "Thank You, Lord" stuck in our throats.

Waves of grief bounced off the walls of our hearts like a tennis ball rebounding with even more force on its return. I wanted to blame someone, but there was no one.

Then the questions started: Could we have prevented it or caught it sooner? Should we have stayed home with her?

Early the next morning we began the somber trip home.

When we picked up Simon from the kennel, he expected to see Bailey in the backseat of the truck.

It was empty.

At home he searched every room.

No Bailey.

He tried to find her trail in the woods.

She wasn't there.

He looked under the deck. But his friend was gone.

For weeks, Simon continued his sorrowful search for Bailey. Every opening door brought a look of anticipation, then disappointment when she wasn't there.

Then, one day he simply stopped looking. It seemed he knew she wasn't coming back. It was time to move on.

We all handle grief differently. Most of us get a lump in our throats when we remember a lost loved one. Some folks grieve a loss for months, others for years—it's a personal process.

I heard a friend say, "Life is like a bus. It stops to let some people get on and others get off, but the bus keeps moving." That's life.

Alfred Lord Tennyson said it best. "Tis better to have loved and lost than never to have loved at all." If we truly love, we will truly grieve.

Life is a gift from God, and so is love. Let's make the most of both.

King David wrote, "The life of mortals is like grass, they flourish like a flower of the field; the wind blows over it and it is gone, and its place remembers it no more. But from everlasting to everlasting the Lord's love is with those who fear him." (Psalm 103:15-17) God understands the pain of loss and He grieves too. But He promises one day there will be no more death or mourning.[3] And that's a day I'm looking forward to.

I've gotten beyond the pain of losing Bailey—mostly. Grief has been pushed aside by gratefulness and I remember her with tenderness and affection.

It's time to move on. You may not think animals will be in Heaven, but I believe I'll see her again. Once again she'll be galloping through the fields and exploring the woods until the shadows grow long.

---

[3] Revelation 21:4.

Now I can truly say, "Thank You, Lord, for the time You gave me with my precious almond-eyed girl."

***

Have you lost a loved one? Where are you in the grieving process?

But you, God, see the trouble of the afflicted; you consider their grief and take it in hand (Psalm 10:14).

Chapter 10 – The Cat

"Cats are the ultimate narcissists. You can tell this because of all the time they spend on personal grooming. Dogs aren't like this. A dog's idea of personal grooming is to roll on a dead fish." — James Gorman

Our house came with a cat. The previous owners had a tomcat named Mittens and their parting words to us were, "Here's a bag of cat food. We'll be back to get him next week when we get settled in." *Yeah, right.*

Three months later Mittens was firmly established as an outdoor member of our family. Bailey pretty much ignored the mouser and when Simon came to live with us he did too. Mittens avoided the two by positioning himself on higher ground, sneering at their dog-play with disdain, like royalty looking down on commoners. Occasionally Simon would notice the furry feline and move in for a sniff. The clever cat tolerated these intrusions. He never tried to start a fight but he was always ready to finish it if "that dumb dog" overstepped.

One summer Mittens disappeared. "Maybe he's found another home, one without dogs," I suggested as I looked out the kitchen window to where he would perch in the evenings. Simon and Bailey hadn't noticed his absence.

That fall as we were sitting with company on the back porch one evening, Mittens returned. He had lost about five pounds and was in obvious agony as he crept down the hill toward us. We could see his ribs under his skin and his fur had a reddish cast as if he had been bleeding. Simon and Bailey looked up as if to say, "Oh, it's you. Have you been gone?"

We set out food and water and remade his bed for him, but he wasn't interested.

He climbed up to sit in his usual spot on the kitchen windowsill that evening, but was gone the next morning.

The next evening he returned with his same labored steps. "He needs to see the vet," Suki said.

So we prayed, "Lord, if You want us to keep Mittens and take care of him, bring him back tomorrow during regular office hours." Although he wasn't technically ours, we felt responsible for him. Even so, we didn't want to pay an additional emergency room bill.

The next day Mittens showed up in the afternoon. We called Dr. Amy.

"How are we going to carry him?" I asked Suki. "He won't sit still for a fifteen-minute ride in the truck."

"We'll put him in a pillowcase so he won't squirm too much."

I picked up our ailing kitty and started to put him in the pillowcase when Suki took a second look at the cat in my hands. "Hey, didn't Mittens have a scar on his nose?"

"Yes," I looked at the cat's scarless nose.

"And didn't he have a big chunk taken out of his ear?"

I looked more closely at the stranger in my hands. "This isn't Mittens!"

"Well, he must be his son or a twin." *How could we have possibly missed that?*

When we got to the vet's office the attendant asked, "What's the cat's name?"

Suki and I looked at one another as if we were reading each other's mind, "Ditto," we said in unison.

Dr. Amy took one look at the cat and said, "We should test him for feline leukemia before we start any treatment. If he has that, there's no point in doing anything else."

She took some blood and returned a few minutes later. "Well, Kitty," she said, "it's your lucky day!" She turned to us, "He doesn't have leukemia, but we'll need to keep him for a day or two," Dr. Amy added. "He'll need antibiotics and he's dehydrated. He's also infested with fleas. The reddish color on his fur is from flea droppings."

Three days later we picked up our new cat, Ditto. He was clean, alert and friskier.

"He was so infested with fleas, I had to dip him twice," Dr. Amy said. "I'd say he's one or two years old. But since you've invested a bit of money in him now, you should consider getting him neutered. Otherwise, he'll run off again. Give him a couple of weeks to build up his strength, then let me know what you want to do."

Three weeks later he had the surgery and he never left home again.

Ditto adapted to the overall routine easily. While we were gone during the day, he would hang out in the cool woods. When we returned home, he would bound down the hill to say, "hello" and meet us before we even got out of the car. He would spring onto our laps whenever we were sitting on the back porch or around the fire pit. With just a little attention and a rub behind the ears Ditto would curl up beside us and purr like a new lawnmower.

Other than an occasional passing sniff, Simon and Bailey continued to ignore him. However, from time to time, Ditto would slink through Bailey's legs in figure-eight rubs. Bailey didn't mind.

When Bailey died, Simon lost his playmate and Ditto lost his quiet companion. In their grieving, Simon and Ditto turned to one another.

Soon Ditto was figure-eighting his way through Simon's legs and Simon was licking Ditto's ear until the side of his small face was soaked. Simon and Ditto had become friends.

Dogs and cats are supposed to be natural enemies. Most dogs like to chase small animals (like cats) and most cats don't like sudden loud noises (like barking dogs). Both are carnivorous predators and in the wild are often competing for the same food source (like mice). On the other hand, dogs are social. They often come right up to a new person to investigate; while cats are isolationists and typically hang back to assess the situation before stepping forward.

It seems to me the animosity between dogs and cats is more of a difference of personalities than natural hatred. After all, they're both domesticated animals but they're as different as, well, cats and dogs.

Sometimes it's easy to look at people who are different, too, and automatically make negative assumptions about them. We want everyone to be the same/equal. The only problem is we're not. We've become a people of narrow-minded separatists: men vs. women, rich vs. poor, black vs. white, patriot vs. objector, young vs. old, vegan vs. meat eater, SEC vs. Pack 10. We all occasionally find ourselves pointing a finger at the one who's different. The world calls it intolerance. The Bible calls it judging—and Jesus doesn't like it.

In His most famous discourse and possibly His first public sermon recorded in Matthew 7, Jesus says, "Do not judge, or you too will be judged. For in the same way you judge others, you will be judged, and with the same measure you use, it will be measured to you." He makes it clear, there's only One who's qualified to judge—and it's not you or me.

You see, our judgments of one another are incomplete and inaccurate. They are based on appearances, actions, situations and consequences. We can't see into someone's heart, nor can we know the complete history that shaped attitudes and behavior.

Only God can.

Instead of passing judgment on one another, let's take the time to get to know folks who look and think differently. We'll be challenged, certainly, but we may also gain some understanding. Who knows, we may even end up finding a bit of tolerance around the corner.

Simon and Ditto didn't judge one another. They accepted their differences and got to know each other. Now they enjoy one another's company. Isn't it time we did the same?

But please, don't lick my ear!

***

Are you guilty of judging? Do you need to ask God's forgiveness?

Therefore judge nothing before the appointed time; wait until the Lord comes. He will bring to light what is hidden in darkness and will expose the motives of the heart. At that time each will receive their praise from God (1 Corinthians 4:5).

Chapter 11 – Built to Please

"Man is a dog's idea of what God should be." — *Holbrook Jackson*

Foxes don't make good pets. Of course, in my opinion neither do boa constrictors, alligators or lizards. But there's no accounting for folks' preferences.

Interestingly, there's a group in Russia which has been trying to domesticate foxes as house pets since 1959.[4] So if you wanted a fox as a pet back then, all you needed was approval to import a certified domesticated animal into the United States and $8000. Seeing the profit potential, other fox breeders have popped up since then, so apparently pet foxes aren't as rare as they once were. If you're interested, today you can purchase one for as little as $400.

There's only one problem. Foxes aren't dogs. While these wild animals can be "domesticated,"

---

[4] Dan Nosowitz, Can I Have a Pet Fox? (January 23, 2013).

they don't fit into the family well because they have no desire to please their masters. They are beautiful animals, but their inability to adjust to house living makes for a pretty poor pet. You can train them not to bite you, but they will never cuddle up to you while you're watching TV or look you in the eye. Here's why: they're loners and they're naturally *wild* animals!

Dogs, on the other hand, are social animals. They adopt the family as their pack and have a built-in disposition to love and please their masters.

Our canine companions are overjoyed to see us when we come home and they miss us when we're away. And talk about wanting to please—all I have to say to Simey is, "Good boy" and like windshield wipers set on automatic, his tail takes on a life of its own. As a child looks for praise, Simon looks to Suki and me for approval. He moves in for a pat on the head whenever he does something he knows will please us. As big as he is, Simon will flop down next to my chair because, unlike a fox, he wants to be close.

This devotion to their masters makes dogs want to protect and please. Have you ever seen a Chihuahua nip at a grown person 30 times its size because that person was too near his master? Or have you seen a 90-pound dog roll over or sit because his master spoke a command?

When Suki and I go away for a few days, we don't have to worry that Simon will shift his allegiance to the dog sitter. While he likes her, he's not devoted to her. He simply treats her like a guest in his home. He'll be polite and will do what she asks but she is not his master.

Loyalty isn't "learnable." It's an overflow of the heart. And believe me, dogs have a lot of heart. No matter how many rewards you give a fox, you can't train him to be loyal. If you let a fox outside without a leash, he'll be gone—and you'll be out $8000!

I think God put a loyalty gene in our furry friends' DNA on purpose. A dog's devotion to his master is the perfect illustration of how Christ-followers should be.

In his biography of Jesus, Luke tells the story of two sisters, Mary and Martha. Jesus had come for a visit with His disciples and Martha was in the kitchen trying to cook and set the table. Instead of helping her sister, Mary chose to sit at Jesus' feet. I imagine her listening intently to Jesus' latest stories, content to be near Him. I can picture Martha storming into the room with a dishtowel in one hand and a spoon in the other. She's angry because her sister isn't helping, so she complains to Jesus, hoping He'll scold Mary for not helping in the kitchen. Instead, He says, "Martha, Martha, you are worried and upset about many things, but few things are needed—or indeed only one. Mary has chosen what is better and it will not be taken away from her."[5]

I don't think Jesus is scolding Martha as much as He is saying loyalty isn't always demonstrated in the doing. Sometimes, it's in the being—like sitting at His feet or strolling beside Him on the trail. While work and service are important, God doesn't want us to spend all our time in the kitchen. Instead, He simply wants us to sit with Him. After all, isn't that what friends do?

Not only does Jesus recognize loyalty, He rewards it. Jesus speaks to the churches about the last days in Revelation 2 & 3. He warns us about the difficult days ahead and encourages us with the words, "To him who overcomes ... I will give ..." Loyalty to our King will bring its own reward. So I have determined to remain loyal to Jesus, no matter what. I will not betray Him, even if times get hard. I have set my heart on my King because He is the reward and I want to be near Him. Beyond that nothing else matters.

Sadly, some think loyalty is old-fashioned. They see a dog-eat-dog world out there and always "take care of number one." To "get ahead" they will betray confidences, break their word or exaggerate to make themselves look better.

Another word for loyalty is faithfulness. God delights in faithfulness from His children because He was faithful to us first. He set a plan in motion

---

[5] The proper translation is found in Luke 10:38-42.

for our redemption before the beginning of time. Starting with Adam, God made a series of promises or covenants with us that He will not break.

The final covenant was sealed with His Son's blood. At the Last Supper recorded in Luke 22, Jesus said, "This cup is the new covenant in my blood, which is poured out for you." When we take communion we are declaring our loyalty all over again.

God has never abandoned us and He never will. He's our creator and that alone positions us (the created) to be the loyal subjects. However, instead of demanding our loyalty, He promises to reward those who remain true to Him.

Simey's not fooled by the dog sitter. He knows who his master is.

Do we?

***

Where do your loyalties lie? Do you need to re-prioritize them?

My eyes will be on the faithful in the land, that they may dwell with me (Psalm 101:6).

Chapter 12 – The Scent

"Dogs are miracles with paws.'— Attributed to Susan Ariel Rainbow Kennedy

"Simon! ..." I waited, then called again. "Si—mey! ..."

The leaves rustled, and I caught a glimpse of our honey-colored lab sprinting toward the house from the pond. With his tail held high and his ears flapping he charged ahead, rounding the bench like a home-run hitter passing third base and heading in for the score.

Suddenly, as if some unseen leash was yanking him, Simon skidded to a halt and veered sharply to the right. I peered out to the field to see what had captured his attention. All I could see was tall grass waving at me.

I looked back at the dog. With his tail standing at attention, his nose was to the ground following a trail only he could "see." His nose, not his eyes or ears, led him this way and that. I watched in fascination as he zigzagged through the yard like a hummingbird flirting with a feeder. Simon didn't

79

mind that the circuitous trail was taking him nowhere. He was totally focused on reading the smells. Even my calling didn't deter him.

Obviously Simon could smell something I couldn't. Canines have up to 300 million olfactory receptors in their noses; humans only have about six million. A Barnard College researcher made this comparison: If we can smell one teaspoon of sugar in a cup of coffee, a dog could detect the same amount of sugar in a million gallons of water.[6]

When hounds breathe, their noses take in air from the front and expel it out the slits in the sides. That way they can track the subtlest of smells without blowing away the scent when they exhale. Those mutts can even tell whether the scent is coming into their right or left nostril, so they turn accordingly.[7]

Dog owners have learned to make use of their animals' amazing olfactory abilities in many ways. Canine cops sniff through millions of suitcases looking for a single zip-lock bag of illegal drugs. Rescuers use our furry friends to track people who are lost. Police and military personnel trust their ability to sniff out bombs, and now scientists are experimenting with the idea that some dogs can

---

[6] Peter Tyson, Nova, "Dogs' Dazzling Sense of Smell,"(October, 2012).
[7] Nova, Ibid.

smell both early and late-stage lung and breast cancer.[8]

So when Simon catches the scent of something and heads off to find the source, I know he's following something real, even though I can't see it or smell it.

When I was a kid, my mom would say, "Something doesn't smell right." Besides describing last night's dinner scraps rotting in the garbage, she was often explaining the feeling she had when something was wrong. Like a seismograph detecting the slightest tremor underground, she caught me in more than one lie.

Some of us can sense when something is wrong, while the rest of us literally trip over a problem before we notice anything amiss.

Sherlock Holmes, the world's most famous consulting detective, created by Sir Arthur Conan Doyle, solved crimes by using a keen sense of observation. He could look at a stranger and often tell where they worked, where they lived, and even what they had for lunch. It wasn't a magic trick. He gathered information by observing, sniffing and even tasting. He had trained himself to notice the little things, like a hair on a jacket, the frayed edges of a shirt sleeve or calluses on a hand, etc.

There's another layer of observation beyond frayed shirt sleeves and calluses that Holmes never

---

[8] Can Dogs Smell Cancer? Science News, (SAGE Publications, January 6, 2006).

investigated. It's spiritual understanding. The Bible calls it discernment, and God says it's a skill that can be developed. (Hebrews 5:14) Spiritual discernment grows like our muscles do. The more we use it, the stronger it will become.

In Ephesians 6, Paul says our fight isn't against people; it's against the supernatural forces affecting those people. Discernment is learning to identify those forces.

We can't smell things like dogs do, but we all can learn to recognize the "spiritual scents" around us. Let me illustrate. Have you ever entered a room where two people have been arguing? There's a chill in the air (It's not the temperature.) and your"nose" picks it up. Or have you ever stepped into a store that felt creepy? Your discernment was kicking in telling you to move on.

Sometimes we know something's wrong, but we can't identify it. That's where we need God's help. His Holy Spirit can give us an understanding and nudge us to choose the appropriate response.

It could be someone is asking you to do something and you don't feel right about it. Perhaps you hear a story that doesn't sound like the truth. Maybe someone is approaching on the sidewalk and you have a sense you should cross the street to avoid him. All those feelings are what some folks call a sixth sense or intuition. To others, it's instinct or following a hunch. To Christ-followers it's discernment or "Spirit-led wisdom."

Whatever we call it, we all need it.

Sometimes the thing we "smell" is sweet, like a spring bouquet, and instead of scampering in the opposite direction, the scent draws us in. Do you know folks you enjoy being with? Maybe it's their smile, or the look in their eyes, the things they say or because they're comfortable. Whatever it is, it's attractive. Those folks leave a "scent" you want to follow. In 2 Corinthians 2:15 Paul says, "For we are to God the pleasing aroma of Christ among those who are being saved and those who are perishing."

He encouraged people to follow the scent of Jesus. Unlike Simon, who will go hither and yon following various scents, we are called to stay with the scent and follow permanently.

Christ-followers chase after a scent the world can't explain. It may look like we're moving in circles, and sometimes we are, but if the scent leads me toward Jesus, that's one I want to follow.

Hold on ...

I caught a whiff of something ...

***

How's your spiritual sense of smell? What scents are you following?

The wise in heart are called discerning, and gracious words promote instruction (Proverbs 16:21).

Chapter 13 – Fireworks!

"Let sleeping dogs lie."—Robert Walpole

"Scaredy" describes cats, not dogs.

Simon acts like he's not afraid of anything. He naps on the porch in the middle of a storm with lightning flashing and thunder crashing. If I'm cleaning house, the drone of the vacuum cleaner doesn't bother him. I have to nudge him with it to get him to move. He doesn't even shiver around strangers and he has never been one to hide under the bed or stand in the corner trembling in fear.

He does, however, have a problem with fireworks. I don't think they make sense to him. A high-pitched whine pierces his ears while a streak of light shoots heavenward. An explosion rocks the atmosphere and colored sparks fall toward the earth like raindrops dripping from trees. No matter how fast he races or how high he jumps, he can't catch those unnatural lights.

We bought dog tranquilizers when we lived in the city to help Simey through local celebrations. Every Fourth of July it seemed all the kids in the neighborhood were competing to see who had the greatest aerial display. Firecrackers answered one another around the block like enemy artillery in battle.

We'd turn up the volume on the TV, hold our Simey-Boy close and pray the tranquilizers were working. With each sizzle and pop he would scurry from Suki to me, panting and panicked.

A few years ago it rained on Independence Day. There were no fireworks outside and no dramatic episodes inside. We had made it safely through another holiday—or so we thought.

The next night we headed to a meeting and left Simon in the fenced-in backyard. When we got home, Simon was at the back door with terror-filled eyes and bloodied lips. He had chewed through the molding and pulled the framing loose around the glass panes of the French door. Even the metal doorknob had teeth marks on it!

Our neighbors had made up for all the celebrations they had missed the night before with extra doses of pyrotechnics. Judging by all the red confetti in the streets, the neighborhood must have sounded like a two-hour bombing assault.

Our carefree pooch changed that day. The unfamiliar spirit of fear crept into his heart and Simon lost his bravado. From then on, he never wanted to be left alone. We had to lure him outside if he thought we were leaving. When we returned, he greeted us with his head down and tail between his legs. Anxiety darkened his personality. He became suspicious, clingy and uncertain.

When we moved to the country permanently, with no fireworks or fenced-in back yards, anxiety gradually left Simon. With renewed confidence he became king of his domain again. Now when we drive off he fearlessly stands at the head of the driveway watching us. On our return, he's usually napping on the front porch or in the shade of a tree calmly waiting for us.

We all have explosions in our lives—times of unexpected fireworks that leave a crater anxiety wants to fill. Loud bangs like a waiter dropping a glass in a restaurant or two cars colliding on the street come without warning and make our hearts skip a beat. A broken glass won't keep me from eating out, but a bad accident might suspend my driving for a time. Uneasiness is a valid emotion if it stays within healthy boundaries. I mean if you're staring into the face of a bear who's licking his lips, your heart should be thumping.

Unchecked, unease can lead to anxiety. When concern morphs into "fear" we've crossed a spiritual line.

Our circumstances overwhelm us and we stop focusing on the One Who overcomes them. For example, the disciples thought they saw a ghost on the Sea of Galilee one night when Jesus approached them walking on the water. We read that casually, but if I saw someone standing on the TOP of a lake, I'd be freaked out too!

Jesus asked Peter to join Him ON THE WATER so he boldly threw his foot over the side of the boat. Peter's bravery sustained him on his liquid carpet until he stopped looking at Jesus. Fear overcame him and he began to sink. However, before criticizing Peter for his lack of faith, let's remember he was the only one who got out of the boat!

There's one thing I'm sure of: life is uncertain. Our lives can be redirected in the blink of an eye or with one phone call. Everything shifts, like two tectonic plates colliding, and on the heels of those tremors Fear sticks its foot in the door.

Over 13 percent of Americans are taking some type of anti-anxiety medication.[9] Is our world that scary? For many the answer is "Yes." We are becoming increasingly isolated, substituting social media for real relationships. Our lives shrink down to the screens on our devices contributing to the rise of social anxiety among teenagers. Computers connect, but they can also disconnect.

We're easy prey if the enemy can isolate us. When tigers or wolves attack a herd, they separate one animal from the rest and gang up on it. The enemy works the same way. If we're isolated, we lose perspective and Fear becomes the loudest voice in our head.

---

[9] Justin Karter, Percentage of Americans on Antidepressants Nearly Doubles, (November 6, 2015).

Fear shrinks our world down to the size of a fenced-in backyard. Yet Scripture tells us we have not been given a spirit of Fear, but of sound mind.

God says perfect love casts out all fear. In other words He, Who is perfect love, can remove all our fear. If we give our fear to Him, He can replace it with peace.

Let's cast aside fear and embrace the world around us. Like the tee shirt says, "Life is good,"[10] and I don't want to be scratching at the back door to come inside when the warm sun is shining and the smell of flowers is in the air.

After all, "scardy" isn't for me either.

***

What are you afraid of? Why don't you give your fear to God and let His peace fill your heart?

So do not fear, for I am with you; do not be dismayed, for I am your God. I will strengthen you and help you; I will uphold you with my righteous right hand (Isaiah 41:10).

---

[10] Life is Good Company, founded in 1989 by Bert and John Jacobs.

Chapter 14 – Scratching an Itch

"If you lie down with dogs, you get up with fleas."—attributed to Benjamin Franklin

"STOP SCRATCHING!"

Simon's hind foot digs behind his ear, jingling the tags on his collar like keys on a chain. The commotion is a noisy interruption of my serious writing! Of course, I've completely ignored the fact that Simey is *seriously* itching. He has a flea.

Anyone who has a dog or cat must deal with the problem of fleas. As cute as they may be in a circus, fleas are some nasty blood-sucking pests. (Personally, I think they're in the same category as mosquitoes, roaches and ringworms—a consequence of the Fall of man in the Garden.)

An adult flea living comfortably in the soft dense forest of your dog's fur can lay up to 30 eggs a day, so in a week one flea can quickly turn into hundreds. Those eggs will usually fall off your pet into their bedding, the carpet, the yard and even the cracks in your hardwood floor. In isolation they grow into larvae and form a cocoon where they wait for your innocent four-footed friend to pass by. When the soon-to-be-flea detects heat, vibrations and exhaled carbon dioxide around them, they break out of their cocoons and jump onto their host using their strong back legs, beginning the cycle all over again. If left untreated our houses can become infested.

Flea saliva causes their bites to itch. It can also carry some viruses and even the eggs of tapeworms. Some dogs are allergic to those microscopic vampires and develop dermatitis. The constant scratching can also lead to major skin infections as well as anemia from blood loss. This pea-sized pest can leave lots of damage behind.

But all is not lost. There are effective ways to keep your pet flea-free: shampoos, flea collars, topical treatments and medications that kill the insects at the first bite.

Even though we humans don't usually have fleas, we do have other small pests waiting to attack us in the most unlikely places. Scripture has two names for those tiny tormenters: fiery darts and little foxes. In Ephesians 6 the apostle Paul talks about putting on the armor of God and using the shield of faith to quench all the "fiery darts" from the wicked one. (NKJV)

Flea-like fiery darts are the minor irritations that can jump on us without warning when we're simply going about our daily routines. You know what I mean—a spilled cup of coffee, a flat tire, an unkind word at the office, tripping over shoes left by the back door. There are a gazillion different darts waiting to fly, and once they hit their mark they begin to itch. Like a flea-bite, as we scratch that itch, those minor irritations can fester into major disturbances and become infected.

It's a subtle and clever attack because instead of looking out for others, we become totally self-absorbed with our own scratching. Our focus has shifted inward and those little darts have created a poison cloud that circles around us like a mini-tornado. Not only does it blur our vision, it contaminates everything and everyone we touch.

While darts hit and sting, little foxes nibble. I don't know about you but when I'm crabby, my self-talk spirals downward and I begin to grumble to everyone around me. (nibble, nibble) Instead of taking my hurts to Jesus, who is the ultimate healer, I pick at that scab until my minor irritation becomes a major problem and my nibbling has gnawed up an entire day.

For thirty-three years Jesus lived in our disorderly world so He understands the temptation to pick up a dart and throw it back—which may get rid of the dart, but doesn't solve the problem. Instead, He offers us a sure-fire solution to flaming darts and foxy fault-finding: forgiveness. It's a medicated collar that keeps offenses to a minimum. If we learn to forgive when an offensive dart lands, it can't penetrate our skin and leave its poison, so it falls to the ground like a dead flea.

93

Forgiveness is an effective defense against the enemy's sneaky strategy, but it's more than a one-and-done treatment. It should become an every day, all-the-time, unending lifestyle for us. In Matthew 18, Peter asked Jesus, "Lord, how many times shall I forgive my brother or sister who sins against me? Up to seven times?"

Peter thought he was being generous since the custom of the law only required you to forgive up to three times. But Jesus surprised him when He replied, "I tell you, not seven times, but seventy-seven times." In other words, when the same dart from the same person repeatedly hits us in the same place, instead of scratching we need to forgive, and forgive, and forgive …

Personally, I roll my eyes at that kind of grace, as I'm sure Peter did 2,000 years ago. It seems Jesus is asking us to do the impossible. After all, some of us have suffered horrible violations that clawed at us more like bear attacks than flea bites. Surely those offenses can't be forgiven. Isn't revenge a better option?

Actually, it's not. Revenge is about getting even—paying back what is due—an eye for an eye. But if you put out my eye and in return I take yours out, I'm still blind in one eye. And while we may think revenge will make us feel better, it only lasts a millisecond—like scratching an itch. Revenge is not a permanent fix. Forgiveness is.

Of course, forgiveness won't bring back your eyesight, but it will restore your vision. By forgiving the one who offended us we maintain a balanced perspective. We're freed from the bondage that distorts everything we see.

I know folks who have nibbled at old wounds so long they've forgotten what started the problem in the first place. They're not speaking to their sons or daughters or in-laws, but they can't tell you why. My heart breaks for them because they've nibbled so long the family is wrecked. Where's the grace? The mercy? The forgiveness?

When I look at my own transgressions and see the magnitude of Jesus' suffering to erase those sins, how can I possibly refuse to forgive anyone who has offended me? In light of His sacrifice, I'll do my darnedest to deal with those fiery darts and little foxes when they come.

I don't know about you, but I'm buckling up my own flea collar—just in case.

***

What small darts plague you? Are you quick to forgive?

Catch for us the foxes, the little foxes that ruin the vineyards, our vineyards that are in bloom (Song of Songs 2:15).

Chapter 15 – Barking at Shadows

"Dogs teach us a very important lesson in life: The mailman is not to be trusted"—Sian Ford

I'm in the middle of a wonderful dream. "Congratulations," the game show MC says. "You've won a brand new car!" I shriek with excitement. I'm celebrating my great luck when I look at the television audience. They're all whining. *Whining?*

What? My new car suddenly fades away as I roll over and see Simon sitting politely by my bed staring at me. He's whining, too. I close my eyes hoping he hasn't noticed I'm awake, but I've already lost that game.

He stands, tail wagging as he looks at me with those big brown eyes and whines—again.

"Okay, I'm coming."

Simon is already dancing at the door to my bedroom in eager anticipation. I can barely get it open before he goes bounding down the hall straight to the front door. As I reach for the handle he's bouncing on all fours, like Tigger in *Winnie the Pooh.* With a crack in the opening, Simey's gone like a flash, as if his life depended on it. I watch as he trots to the middle of the front yard and stops short.

Then it starts—the barking. I look around. Nothing's amiss. There are no deer in the field and no rabbits or squirrels in the yard—unlike me, they're still sleeping. As far as I can tell Simon's not barking at anything.

While it looks like Simon is simply barking for show, I think there is purpose to his thunder. According to animal behaviorists, canines bark for all kinds of reasons: to sound an alarm, claim territory, gain attention or because they're frustrated or ill, or because their masters are leaving or coming home. They also bark for social reasons only understood in the canine community.

I tend to forget Simey sees the world differently from me. Like most humans, when I take in information about my surroundings, the primary source I tap into is my sense of sight. The other four senses usually lag far behind. Sight is so dominant in humans we will use it to interpret information from our other senses. How often have we declared, "I have to see it to believe it?"

Dogs, on the other hand, rely less on sight and more on sounds and smells. While I only hear sounds in the 20 to 20,000 Hertz range, Simon can hear ultrasonic frequencies between 40 to 60,000 Hertz. His ears can pick up the squeak of a mouse in the field or the rustling of wild critters in the woods. His nose is also more sensitive than mine so he may be barking at the smell of an animal that recently trespassed in our yard.

He's "seeing" things I cannot. Violet is the color of the highest frequency the human eye can see, but there are ultraviolet colors, or "beyond violet" frequencies that creatures like bees and dogs can see. So, seeing simply can't be the ultimate truth meter in our lives. After all, I can't "see" electricity, but I sure do use it.

The spirit realm is also something we can't see; however, it's as real as the things we can see and touch every day. We live in a multi-dimensional world where the spiritual aspect is interwoven with the physical side like a braided cord. Both realms, although on different wavelengths, work together and influence each other.

God's Word gives us some clues about this unseen realm that are worth exploring. First, God is spirit. (John 4:23-24) He's not an old man with a long white beard scowling down at earth like Zeus. Because He is spirit, He can be everywhere and know everything—all at once. He's not limited by time and space.

Scripture also gives us some clues about what goes on in this unseen realm—a battle. God's angels are constantly confronting the devil's armies in accordance with our prayers and God's directions.

As I learn to use my spiritual senses I can identify ungodly shadows like greed, hostility, fear, rebellion or manipulation. Once I recognize them, I can rebuke them. James says it like this: Submit yourselves, then, to God. Resist the devil and he will flee from you. (James 4:7)

One of the most amazing results of Jesus' death and resurrection was the authority He gave us over spiritual forces. Even though we can't see it, when a Christ-follower speaks, the spirit realm listens.

Too often I hear believers say things like, "The devil's beating me up today."

Without making light of their problem, I often ask, "Why? Have you given him access in some way or are you simply unaware of your own authority?" The enemy wants us to think those shadows are simply figments of our imaginations. His strategy is to cause us to doubt ourselves or, more importantly, doubt his existence.

In the book of Ephesians Paul was writing to a young church established in a city famous for its temple to a pagan goddess, Artemis. The Ephesians knew spiritual power was real. What they didn't know was whether God's power was greater.

Paul begins his letter by reminding them of their adoption into the family of Christ and the spiritual blessings that are theirs. He gives them instructions for living victorious lives amid attacks from the enemy.

He ends his letter with the illustration of a Roman suit of armor, telling them they are protected from unseen oppression. He reminds them to stand firm and to remember their battle is against spiritual forces, not flesh and blood. It's knowing who you're fighting that gives you the advantage.

As Christ-followers we fight with tools like faith, the Word of God and prayer. To the world it probably looks like we're simply barking at shadows. However ...

I'm confident when Christ-followers bark, shadows flee.

***

Are you in a spiritual battle? Are you fighting with spiritual weapons or physical ones?

For our struggle is not against flesh and blood, but against the rulers, against the authorities, against the powers of this dark world and against the spiritual forces of evil in the heavenly realms (Ephesians 6:12).

Chapter 16 – Can I Have a Treat?

"If you think dogs can't count, try putting three dog biscuits in your pocket and then give him only two of them."—Phil Pastoret

It's Christmas, and I can't help but think of Santa Claus. In the United States Christmas has morphed into a Winter Holiday celebrating presents and the jolly man in the red suit who brings them. Santa has supplanted Jesus in many hearts.

Even many Christians think of God as a kindly Santa Claus as we ask for treat after treat, which brings me to my four-legged furry elf, Simey-Boy.

Simon loves treats. What dog doesn't?

As I open the dog biscuits, Simon comes bounding into the kitchen like a kid bouncing down the stairs to see what Santa has left under the tree. With tail at attention and a toothy doggie smile, his eyes are locked on my hand.

He knows what's in it—a goodie. However, there are rules to getting a treat and Simon had to learn them. "No jumping" was the first requirement. That's a hard one for a puppy who is full of energy and excitement.

"Sit" was the second command. Sit, Stay and Come are basic commands for most pups. Simon is the exception. He has the "Sit" and "Come" part pretty well, but doesn't like the "Stay" part. Not his fault, it's our faulty training.

The final stipulation was: "Gently." Simon is a big dog with substantial teeth. The last thing I want is him grabbing at my outstretched hand. I hold the treat in my closed hand until he relaxes. When I open my hand, the treat disappears like lint sucked up by a vacuum cleaner.

Then Simon waits. He knows one treat is usually followed by a second. As mom used to say about cookies, "One for each hand." After the second, he looks for a third—ever hopeful.

That silly dog would ignore his food and eat a whole bag of treats if we didn't set a limit. A diet of only "rewards" isn't good for him.

Truthfully, aren't we all like that too?

For me, it's chocolate and chips. How I wish I could hopscotch from appetizers straight to dessert—with nothing wholesome in between. My brain and taste buds are constantly at war over healthy choices or sweet treats.

God gave us a brain to discern what and how much we should eat. In Deuteronomy, God lays out a reward system of blessings and curses based on relationship with Him and obedience. Both lists begin with: "If." It's a little word with huge Kingdom consequences.

Deuteronomy 28 begins, "*If* (emphasis mine)you fully obey the Lord your God and carefully follow all his commands I give you today, the Lord your God will set you high above the nations on earth." Then the next eleven verses list all the rewards God promises for our obedience.

The only problem is we have a tiny rebellious streak in us that resists having anyone (even God) tell us how to live. We're like Simon when he ignores the "Stay" command. We disregard God's guidelines and run straight into trouble.

Our small compromises and acts of disobedience block our blessings. The catalog of curses for disobedience begins in Deuteronomy 28:15 and continues for over 50 verses. God's not being a bully; He simply knows that bad choices bring about bad fruit.

Let's look at the Israelites. God wanted to bless them. He orchestrated their exodus from slavery in Egypt loaded down with the Egyptians' gold and jewels. He destroyed Israel's enemies. He taught the former slaves how to live and govern themselves. He put them in a land where the fields had already been plowed and crops planted, mortgage-free houses were move-in ready and vineyards overflowed with grapes. Even the weather was good. God handed it all to them and all He asked in return was for them to obey His commands.

The Israelites moved in and were grateful—for a while. Then came the small compromises. In one generation they quit teaching God's rules. They stopped praying and started partying. They traded labor for leisure and sweat for sweets.

Within two generations enemies began showing up. The rain stopped. Crops died. Businesses failed. Plans fell through. Relationships disintegrated. The consequences had begun.

God is telling us, "Don't jump." "Sit." "Be gentle."

We've all jumped the gun—trying to leap over obstacles or others, rather than deal with them. Like breaking in line instead of waiting our turn, we're saying, "I'm more important than you." That's pride.

"Sit." Wait on Him—expectantly. Refusing to wait is saying, "I can't trust God, so I'll do it myself." That's unbelief. God's timing is always perfect and so is His plan. If we're willing to wait, we can soar on eagles' wings with Him.

"Be gentle." Care for others as Jesus did. In describing the coming Messiah, Isaiah said, "A bruised reed he will not break, and a smoldering wick he will not snuff out." While Jesus confronted sin, He never destroyed people in the process. Kingdom living is treating others as you would have others treat you. When we don't, it's selfishness.

God loves us all the same, but He rewards us differently—based on our behavior. In Matthew

25, Jesus tells a story of a master who was going on a long journey and entrusted his wealth to three servants. When he returned the servants told him how they had handled the money. What they did with the money determined how he would reward them.

Here's the point: Everything we have has been given to us by God. If we obey Him and steward His gifts well, we will receive a reward. However, God's rewards aren't like the twenty percent tip we give a waiter or the ten percent tip we give Him in church. God says He will give us more than we can hold. (Luke 6:38)

So, the next time you hear the goodie bag rattling, scamper over to God. Don't jump. Sit. Be gentle. His gift is more than you can hope or imagine.

Now that's a reward!

***

Are you working for a reward? Are you compromising any of His rules?

I press on toward the goal to win the prize for which God has called me heavenward in Christ Jesus (Philippians 3:14).

Chapter 17– Rainy Days and Mondays

"The average dog is a nicer person than the average person."—Andy Rooney

"Rainy days and Mondays always get me down"[11] keeps playing through my mind as I lie in my bed and listen to the rain drumming against my bedroom window. I want to roll over and bury my head in the pillows. *Another dreary day,* I sigh. Gray skies drifted in weeks ago and haven't left. I drag myself out of bed and shuffle down the dark hall to get a cup of coffee—fortification against the gloominess. My mood is as soggy as the ground outside.

In contrast, Simon always wakes up in a good mood.

Every morning he opens his eyes, takes a circular tour of his pillow, stretches, shakes his head—spreading dog hairs around the room—and with his tail in the air and a smile on his face, he

---

[11] Rainy Days and Mondays, 1971 by Roger Nichols and Paul Williams, performed by Richard and Karen Carpenter.

trots down the hall ready to go outside. He always gets up on the right side of the bed.

Of course, you could say, he's only a dog and doesn't have any worries, and you might be right. After all, he lives in a house, is well-fed and well-loved. He's not stressed about where the food comes from or whether the bills are paid. However, I think even if he were homeless and had to scrounge for his food, he would be cheerful.

I also believe rescued animals, remembering where they came from, have an additional dose of gratefulness. Simon never pouts because he eats the same dog food day in and day out. He doesn't whine because "there's nothing to do" or fret about the future.

Simey seems to get up each morning looking forward to the day. That's not to say he doesn't have difficult moments—like trips to the vet, confrontations with other dogs or a stern word from Suki or me—but, he doesn't brood on those things. It's as if he's choosing to set his mind on the pluses, not the minuses in life.

The American Kennel Club and most pet owners acknowledge that breeds of dogs have distinct characteristics. Labradors, which are listed in the sporting class, have sweet-natured dispositions. They're fun-loving, devoted and affectionate. Those temperaments are as built-in to the breed as the type of tail they have. So because he is part Lab, Simon is pre-disposed to having a positive personality.

We humans can spin through the whole spectrum of emotions and moods in the span of a few minutes. We spiral downward from concerned to anxious, then fearful, followed by frustrated, working our way to angry, and even spiteful with accelerating speed. We seem to forget we have a brake pedal. Then, as boneheaded as it seems, when we finally do crash into something, we look around and say, "How did I get here?"

Attitudes are a choice. Our circumstances take hold of the wheel and lead us down increasingly narrower roads with fewer and fewer places to turn around. Our emotions and attitudes carry us from event to event, until we end up on a dead-end street where the only option left is to back up.

The other day Suki and I were returning home when we saw dozens of blue flashing lights on the country road ahead. There was no traffic in front of us and the street looked clear so we slowly continued on in spite of the warning signs. Five or six patrol cars were parked on the left shoulder past a bridge and officers were prowling everywhere ignoring the line of traffic building up behind me. The situation looked serious, so I stopped and Suki got out of the car to ask the patrolman if we could continue.

We were told to turn around because there had been an "incident," but with cars bumper-to-bumper we were hemmed in like shoppers outside a store on Black Friday. The officer told us to follow a patrol car that was cautiously backing up past the line of cars behind me.

There was no shoulder and no handy side-road so I made a careful 28-point turn to change my direction before backtracking to take a five-mile detour home. We later learned a man on the FBI's Most Wanted List had crashed his car beyond the bridge during a high-speed chase. The blockade was up until police caught him.

We never know what lies ahead, which is why we need to pay attention to the signs. If I let my emotions lead, they will take me speeding past caution signs without a second glance. While they may not have flashing lights, we've all encountered those warnings: A slight frown. A tear forming in the corner of someone's eye. A sharp turn of the head. A slamming door. Unfortunately, we often charge ahead regardless of the consequences, and before we know it, the damage is done.

In his letter to the Philippians, Paul tells us we have a smorgasbord of attitudes we can select when facing difficulties. He says: "don't be frightened," "value others," "don't grumble," "press on," "stand firm," and "rejoice."

If I may borrow an illustration from Robert Frost's famous poem, "The Road Not Taken,"[12] we often come to forks in the road that require a decision. If we are wise, we will pause a moment

[12] Robert Frost (1874-1963), The Road Not Taken, Mountain Interval, (Henry Holt and Company, 1920).

and weigh the options before rushing headlong into the unknown.

Whenever I focus on the negatives, my emotions will lead me down a dark road that pollutes my thinking and infects my relationships. Before I realize it, I am lost in the forest with no clear way out. Good moods are often the harder, less traveled choice, yet they will lead to straighter roads that will take me to my destinations sooner—unless, of course, I decide to stop and smell the roses along the way.

Knowing my temporary mood could grow into a permanent personality trait, I'm going to follow Simey's example. Tomorrow I'm getting up on the right side of the bed regardless of the weather.

How about you?

***

Are you ruled by your emotions or do you rule them? What are some ways you can apply the brake when you're heading the wrong way?

Finally, brothers and sisters, whatever is true, whatever is noble, whatever is right, whatever is pure, whatever is lovely, whatever is admirable—if anything is excellent or praiseworthy—think about such things (Philippians 4:8).

Chapter 18 – Shedding

*"The majority of cats are very gregarious—
they love each other so much; they enjoy living
together and grooming each other."—Celia
Hammond*

I looked out at the well-dressed group of ladies
and smiled. I had been asked to speak to their
affluent gathering about honey bees and the
Kingdom of God, and all was going well. I had
made a connection with these women and they
seemed to be enjoying me and my message. I
paused for a moment to look down at my notes—
and there it was.

A blond hair! It certainly wasn't my hair and it
wasn't the hair of proof from a crime scene or a
romantic rendezvous. This was one of Simon's
leftovers clinging stubbornly to my black jacket. I
tried to brush it off but the darn thing was
practically woven into the fabric. Ah well, I am a
dog owner.

Simon's favorite doctor, Dr. Amy, has a sign in
the waiting room of her office that reads, "No

outfit is complete without pet hair." Most pet owners would smile and nod in agreement—unless they were speaking at an upscale function like I was today. It seems wherever I go, I'm forever taking a piece of Simon with me.

Suki and I try to keep the loose hairs to a minimum by regularly brushing him on the back porch. In one afternoon we can easily fill a couple of plastic bags with grooming fur. Our four-footed fuzz factory loves to be brushed. However, when we finish the routine, Simon proudly saunters back into the living room, shakes his massive head and we watch in amazement as more hair goes flying.

Simey's hairs drift through the air on their own unmanned mission flights, often landing in cracks and crevices we never knew existed. They lie in wait until we pass by, then pop out from their hiding places and attach themselves to us like metal shavings drawn to a magnet. A lint roller catches most of the hair, but occasionally, like today, a stray hair mysteriously works its way from the floor to my jacket—a gentle reminder of my furry friend.

If you have an animal, you probably have pet hair hiding somewhere because, well, animals shed. Our four-legged housemates can have thinning coats for lots of reasons: poor health, medications, skin irritations and allergic reactions, for example. Of course, some dogs slough off their excess insulators more than others and a few breeds don't lose any hair at all. How I wish Simon were one of those! Dogs also naturally have thinner coats when it's hot. In Simey's case, when temperatures climb to the 60's, his furry fluff comes out by the handfuls. I'm amazed he's not completely bald!

Besides making our pooches soft and cuddly, a dog's coat helps control his body temperature and protect his skin from the sun and other environmental elements. A hound's hair stays the same length because when his hair stops growing it falls out.

The thing is, Simon's not trying to shed. He can't decide when he's going to let go of some hair and when he isn't. If that were so, we could send him outside whenever he had the urge to thin his tresses. Now wouldn't that be handy?

I'm sure that long after Simon has gone to doggie Heaven, we'll be finding follicular reminders of our furry friend.

As Christ-followers we should be leaving a residue of ourselves behind, too. Hopefully, it's not hair! Instead, we carry an essence of the Kingdom of God with us and as we weave in and out of the lives of others, we leave a bit of the Kingdom lingering in the atmosphere wherever we go.

As I mentioned in Chapter 12, some folks simply make us smile. They're easy to be around because they carry an undercurrent of joy with them in the most difficult situations. I'm not talking about individuals who are simply funny—

those folks are called comedians. I'm talking about something deeper.

In the fruit of the Spirit Paul mentions in Galatians, joy is number two. The list is a string of attributes wrapped around Christ-followers like a warm blanket—love, joy, peace, patience, kindness, goodness, faithfulness, gentleness, and self-control. This rich list describes the nature of a Kingdom person. The essence of that fruit grows deeper and wider until it can't help but overflow like water splashing out of a glass, leaving a little something behind.

In Israel, the Pharisees spent lots of money and energy trying to stand out in an agrarian society. They strutted through the crowds in self-centered parades dressed in colorful and expensive clothes to highlight their own importance. When they prayed in church, they used their booming outside voices to illustrate their sanctimonious spirituality. When they gave to the needy, they announced it on the streets with trumpets. (Matthew 6:2-16)

Everything they did was for show, but instead of admiration, it produced the opposite effect. Like passing a police car on the highway when you're speeding, their pompous performances only reminded folks of their own lawlessness.

When the real King strolled the streets of Israel and spoke in their midst, there was no trumpeted parade. Jesus simply left the sweet spirit of love lingering in the air. The religious ones were too busy preening like peacocks to recognize Him, but the desperate ones, the wounded ones, the hungry ones did.

Real Kingdom shedding isn't about making a show of our piety everywhere we go. We don't need to stand on a street corner with a megaphone or hit folks over the head with a Bible to preach the Gospel. Kingdom expansion is more like dropping a few hairs here and there.

As Christ-followers we should be leaving God's calling card with every person we meet—a smile, a "thank you," an encouraging word, a listening ear, an understanding nod, a hug. As we grow closer to God, we'll demonstrate His compassion for His people.

If we set aside time for Him, Jesus will fill us with His love and keep on filling us. The overflow from our intimacy with Him will then infuse the atmosphere around us with a Heavenly aroma. And believe me, people will notice.

Remember Moses? He spent forty days in God's presence on Mt. Sinai. When he came down from the mountain, his face was so bright he had to cover it with a veil. He was carrying such a strong reflection of the Kingdom, people couldn't even look at him. (They didn't have sunglasses back then!)

Remember Peter? After being filled with the Holy Spirit, he spoke to a crowd and 3000 became Christ-followers in one day. The Kingdom in Peter even spilled over to his shadow. People would line up their sick relatives like cords of wood along

Peter's path so when his silhouette passed over them they would be healed.

The Apostle Paul's Kingdom nature was so powerful people would give him handkerchiefs to touch. Those small pieces of cloth were then sent to other folks who needed healing—and when the sick touched the cloth, they were healed.

The more time we spend in His Presence, the more the fruit of His Spirit will shine through us. As Paul says in 2 Corinthians, "And we all, who with unveiled faces contemplate the Lord's glory, are being transformed into his image with ever-increasing glory, which comes from the Lord, who is the Spirit." We should be carrying the Kingdom with us everywhere we go and, like Simon's hairs floating in the air, leaving evidence of Jesus behind.

So instead of trying to brush those "hairs" off, why don't we simply give ourselves a little shake? Let's do a little shedding ourselves and let the Kingdom fall wherever it will.

***

Do you carry the essence of the Kingdom? What fragrances are you leaving behind?

And I pray that you, being rooted and established in love, may have power, together with all the Lord's holy people, to grasp how wide and long and high and deep is the love of Christ, and to know this love that surpasses knowledge—that you may be filled to the measure of all the fullness of God (Ephesians 3:17-19).

Chapter 19 – If You Snooze, You Lose

"A dog teaches a boy fidelity, perseverance, and to turn around three times before lying down."—Robert Benchley

Simon's a good napper. When he's outside waiting for us to come home, he's napping on the front porch. In the evenings when we're home he dozes in front of the fireplace. Another favorite place for a dog snooze is at the living room window with the morning sun warming his back. I've also caught him getting some shut-eye under the table, in his crate, in the car, beside my chair, and occasionally, on his pillow. As a matter of fact, Simon can close his eyes almost anywhere and drift away to doggie dreamland in a mongrel minute. He loves to guard the property, but he's not embarrassed if he's caught napping on the job.

I get a kick out of watching him circle around his pillow, scratching, examining and fluffing it. He pulls it one way to make a lump, then digs at it from the opposite direction to smooth it out. Next, he repeats the process from a different angle. After

If You Snooze, You Lose

a short routine of circling, scratching, sniffing, fluffing and pulling, Simon finally decides it's perfect and flops down in the middle of his pillow which looks exactly like it did when he started!

Simon's doesn't have to be told he needs a nap. When he's tired he simply lays his head on his paws and catches a few ZZZ's. He's not even embarrassed when he wakes himself up snoring.

So, what does he know that we don't?

There's a familiar psalm that might help us understand: "The Lord is my shepherd. I shall not want." (NKJV) Recognize it? Most of us know this one. It's the 23rd Psalm. Unfortunately, because it's so familiar, we often breeze through it without pausing to think about what it's saying.

Note the second line: "He makes me to lie down in green pastures; He leads me beside the still waters. He restores my soul;" Did you catch it? He *makes* me. (Emphasis mine) God knows something about us; we don't want to acknowledge about ourselves: we don't want to rest.

"If you snooze, you lose." Raise your hand if that saying has guided your life. I've got both my hands in the air!

We've made productiveness a badge of honor. We read books on time management and hire life coaches to make us more efficient. Granted, some of us need help getting organized, but since when did we need a coach to teach us how to live? We shouldn't be embarrassed about taking time to rest.

124

When meeting a friend we haven't seen in a while, our first question is, "What have you been doing?"

The answer is always one or two degrees above "Busy." I don't think I've ever heard anyone proudly reply, "You know, I've been taking a few walks lately and sitting on the porch reading, and in between I'm taking a few naps."

We stuff our electronic calendars with back-to-back events with barely time to breathe in between. Whether it's soccer games or conference calls, we never seem to slow down. And if we do get a minute, we meet with a life coach to teach us how to squeeze even more into our days.

I'm not dissing life coaches. Many of us need someone to hold us accountable or create structure in our lives. We like the sense of accomplishment we feel from getting things done.

Busyness is not a new problem. Even in David's day God had to MAKE him lie down. God knew then what we're beginning to discover today: rest is critical to our well-being. Scientists tell us our brains work as hard while we're sleeping as when we're awake. They're simply working in different areas.[13] When we close our eyes and drift into that quiet place, our brains get busy repairing and restoring our bodies. (Did you catch it? Did

---

[13] What Happens in the Brain During Sleep? Scientific American.

you hear the word?) Science is using the same word God uses: Restore. "He *restores* my soul."

We're not machines that can work 24 hours a day. Scientists believe on average we humans need seven to nine hours of sleep a night. When we wake, we're usually refreshed and inspired with new ideas and creative solutions—which is why I like to get up early and write in the morning.

I have another favorite line from one of David's psalms: "Be still and know that I am God." (Psalm 46:10) I live on a seven-acre mini-farm in the country. It's a beautiful piece of property in the rolling hills of Tennessee, but occasionally I have a hard time enjoying it. When I sit on the front porch, I notice the grass needs cutting or the flower bed needs weeding. When I sit on the back porch, I get distracted by the bushes that need trimming or the fallen tree branches I need to pick up.

I'm also not a good napper—although I'm working on it. On my first trip to the Philippines, I noticed many folks quit working after lunch, napped until about 3:00 or 4:00 in the afternoon and then stayed up till after midnight socializing. I thought they were lazy until I had lived there a few weeks. Like all warm-climate-culture folks with little or no air conditioning, Filipinos have learned to work with their environment, not against it. They work in the mornings and evenings in the cooler temperatures and conserve their energy by taking a "siesta" during the heat of the day.

Today in the United States we have climate-controlled buildings and electric lights—and I'm so grateful for these wonderful conveniences. However, those advantages have interrupted our natural life patterns. Like the Filipinos, our great-grandparents rested in the heat of the day and went to bed at sundown when the natural light was gone (and, incidentally, they also got up at sunrise).

God designed our bodies to work with nature and He designed nature to work with us by giving us "night." If we pay attention, our bodies will tell us when we need to take a breather. There's nothing shameful about putting our feet up. We're more efficient when we're rested—and we're in a better position to hear from God.

So why don't you circle the pillow a few times and try it out? I'll even fluff it for you.

***

Is the Lord asking you to take a rest? What are some ways you can adjust your schedule?

The Lord is my shepherd, I lack nothing. He makes me lie down in green pastures, he leads me beside quiet waters, he refreshes my soul (Psalm 23:1-2).

Chapter 20 – Watch Me!

"Dogs travel hundreds of miles during their lifetime responding to such commands as 'come' and 'fetch.'"—Stephen Baker

Suki and I rediscovered the joys of bike riding while on vacation to Biltmore Estate in North Carolina. Within a week of returning home, we decided to buy two bikes to ride around the neighborhood. "It'll be great exercise," I reasoned. "And Simon will love it!"

The next day, helmets in place and tires pumped up, we hit the road. As we pedaled on, I told Suki, "Let's teach Simon to jog alongside the bikes and he'll get some exercise too. I've seen folks roller skate with dogs, so this shouldn't be too hard. We'll have to go slow at first and work out some commands."

I decided to hold his leash in my left hand to keep him away from tempting bushes on my right that might halt our progress. I would hold the leash loosely so if he pulled, I could easily let go and wouldn't end up sporting a full-body cast.

We started the training clumsily walking down the street with Simon on the left, me on the right and the bike in the middle. At the end of the street we turned back. We took the same route because I figured he would have already watered every mailbox in the area and could focus on me. I got on the bike and pedaled slowly with him lumbering by my side. I began to pedal faster and he easily kept up. We were doing fine until we came to the end of the lane and had to turn right or left. *Uh Oh,* I thought. *I need a new command— quick!* I'd forgotten that part of the training. So I said the first thing that came to mind. "Watch me!"

I gave the command as I turned the wheel. The words were new and he didn't understand. He kept trotting straight ahead while I headed right. He zigged and I zagged. I wobbled. He tugged against the leash. I jerked his lead. He came up short. Swiveling the handlebars back and forth to stay upright, I teetered on the brink of face-planting on the asphalt. At the last moment, Simon made the shift and followed to the right.

I made a few more right-hand turns with the same instruction, "Simon ... watch me." After a little work and several seesaw turns, he caught on to the idea. Before long, Simey was following like a pro.

Of course not all streets offer right-turn-only options, which meant we had to work on turning left, too. I didn't want to use a different signal because I have enough trouble remembering the one command, much less two! I wanted to train him to pay attention to what I was doing, not simply respond without thinking.

Once again, I started slowly. As we came to the end of the street I gave the command again. However, this time I began to turn left. Simon, who was simply enjoying the trot and not paying attention, began his automatic turn to the right. Crash! Simon's head slammed into my front wheel and even though we didn't go down like Humpty Dumpty, we stopped moving. Simey looked up at me as if to say, "What are you doing? Don't you know the rules? You're supposed to turn right!"

We had several more collisions before he began to get the hang of it. "Simon ... watch me." Right turn. "Simon ... watch me." Left turn. "Simon ... watch me." Right turn. Soon my trotter and I were making right and left-hand turns easily. I would give the command and he would look at me to see which way the front wheel was turning and adjust his direction. As we continued our practice, I gradually increased my speed. Before long Simey was trotting alongside the bike with ease,in tune to my directions.

I think God uses the same approach with us. He doesn't simply want us to follow the rules blindly without thinking. Scripture calls that living under the law. Our Father wants us to be responsive to Him in every situation.

Have you ever wondered why the Bible sometimes seems to contradict itself? For example

Paul says don't get drunk on wine, yet Jesus turned water into wine. The law says, "An eye for an eye," but Jesus tells us to turn the other cheek. In another instance, Paul says to get married AND to stay single, and to eat meat AND don't eat meat. So, which is it?

I think the "law" is deliberately ambiguous because God wants us to "Watch Him." Why should one get married and another not? Or one eat meat or drink wine and another not? When should we expect compensation for an offense or extend forgiveness? Could it have something to do with God's calling on our individual lives, or the season we're in, or our own self-control?

God knows it's impossible for us to keep His laws. That's why He established a New Covenant with Jesus—a covenant of grace, but that doesn't mean we throw out the rules. God will never lower His standard. What it does mean is when we fall short of the rules we have an option—to ask for forgiveness—which opens the door for communication and a God-relationship. Our Heavenly Father is big enough to have a unique relationship with each of His kids and to give every one of us personal guidelines. I believe He wants us to ask, "God, what do You think? What would You like me to do?"

The first two kings of Israel, Saul and David, are great examples. Saul cared more about how he looked to the people than how he related to God.

He wanted to live life on his own terms. When God's law didn't suit him, he simply broke it.

David came to know God while tending sheep alone in the fields. He talked and sang to the Lord and he listened when God spoke to him. He carried on that relationship even after he became king. When he broke the law, instead of blaming others, he repented because he knew his relationship with God was more important than anything else. David didn't simply live by the law; he spent his life asking the Lord His opinion in every situation. Thus he became "a man after God's own heart."

Blindly following the law will have us banging our head into the front wheel whenever there's a turn in the road. God has a way to keep us in step with Him.

He simply says, "Watch Me."

***

Do you find rules easy to follow? How do they keep you from having a relationship with others—or God?

You who are trying to be justified by the law have been alienated from Christ; you have fallen away from grace (Galatians 5:4).

Chapter 21 – The Escape Artist

"The thing I like most about dogs is their absolute belief in their own innocence, even when they've been caught redhanded. No matter what they've been doing, every bad dog bears the same look when scolded: 'What?'"—Craig Wilson

Simon has learned to open doors—both coming and going. Unfortunately, he still hasn't gotten the hang of closing them yet. We have often returned home after leaving our Houdini outside only to find the front door wide open and Simon lounging on his pillow inside the house!

He first learned this trick to get in and out of the screened-in back porch. In his rush to go outside he didn't want to wait for us to open the back door for him, so he started pushing it open with his head. Once he had figured out how to open the door from the inside, it didn't take long before he started working on the door from the outside.

He started hooking his nails in the ornamental mesh and pulling open the screen door. A four-footed Houdini was discovered! (Has anyone seen my car keys?)

This skill is useful in the spring and fall when we can leave the back door open. Simon can come and go through the porch as he pleases. However, once he understood the concept, he graduated from screened doors to door handles. He figured out if he pushed down on the lever with his paw and pressed against the door with his head, he could get inside. That was the trick he used on the front door.

He's learned the same trick with fences and gates. Once while staying overnight at Dr. Amy's, he broke out of his six-foot enclosure and escaped into the clinic after the staff had left for the evening. He bypassed all the good dog food and treats for sale in bags on the floor. Instead, he made a beeline for the bread someone had left on the counter in the break room. He ate the whole loaf for a midnight snack, peed on the floor in the waiting room, took a nap and waited for someone to show up for work the next morning. We're grateful Dr. Amy and her tolerant staff have a sense of humor.

His funniest escape act happened when we lived in town. Every time Suki and I would leave the house, we put Simon in the fenced-in back yard. We would return home to find him napping on the shady porch or basking in the sun on the grass.

One summer day the two of us headed to town to run a few errands. While we were out, our concerned neighbor called. "Simon's out. He's sitting in the front yard."

We were thirty minutes away. "We'll be right home," I said as we cut our trip short and turned toward the house.

"I'll put him in our garage until you get here," she said.

When we got home, our neighbor came out to meet us.

"I don't know where he went. When I came back outside to get him, he was gone."

Oh no.

"I'll get the keys to the truck," Suki said as she headed into the house. "We'll have to drive through the neighborhood till we find him."

I waited outside with our distraught neighbor. In a minute Suki called from the kitchen door. "You've got to see this."

As I entered, I could see Simon sitting innocently at the glass-paneled back door, pretending he'd been there the whole time we were gone.

"If he broke out of the back yard, how did he break back in?"

"He either pulled the gate open or he jumped the fence," Suki answered.

I looked at Simon. He looked back at us like a guilty teenager. He had cocked his head to one side and was trying to put on the most innocent face as he could muster as if to say, "What?"

When we examined the scene of the crime, we discovered tell-tale evidence of muddy scratches on the back gate. The lock at the top of the gate had given Simon enough room to push the door open at the bottom and squeeze through. We found his escape hatch.

The next day we added another lock to the bottom of the back gate.

Suki and I have no idea how many other times Simon had broken out of the yard and snuck back in without us catching him. We were pretty sure that wasn't his first escape. It was, however, the only time we actually caught him red-handed.

Have you ever been caught red-handed by God? I have. He noticed me signing a document and putting the nice company pen in my purse. He heard me yelling at the old man in the pickup truck ahead of me for not going fast enough. He also saw me criticizing another person because they don't do things my way and choosing to waste an hour on Facebook rather than working on my book.

When God "catches" me, I rationalize. "What? It's a company pen. They give them away for advertising," "What? That guy's too old to drive," "What? My way's more efficient," "What? My brain needs a break."

However, God's not fooled.

He quietly asks, "Did they give that pen to you?"

I'm convicted. According to the dictionary, "Conviction" is the declaration made by a judge in a court of law that someone is guilty of a criminal offense. When I'm convicted, I'm guilty (and I know it). I admired the pen. It felt good in my hand and the ink flowed smoothly. And, after all, I am a writer. I made a decision and I took it. The pen didn't jump into my purse. I put it there. I'm guilty.

What?

I was caught red-handed!

The Holy Spirit tells us when we've sinned. He also gives us a way to fix it: we sometimes couple repentance (asking for forgiveness) with restitution (giving it back).

Conviction, however, isn't the same as condemnation.

The enemy wants to condemn us. He has already passed judgment declaring us guilty, unfit, unredeemable, destitute, bankrupt, spoiled and defeated criminals with no possibility of parole. He points his finger as he accuses us. He wants to torture us with guilt and shame about who we are, not what we've done.

Satan says, "You're an awful person for taking that pen," but he never gives us a way to resolve the issue. He's a seasoned accuser and he knows our weaknesses. His strategy is to get us to believe we're bad at our core and we can't possibly change.

According to the enemy, we might as well give up altogether and make the most of our criminal nature.

On the other hand, God says, "What you did was bad, but all you have to do is repent. I love you and together we can change your heart, which will alter your behavior."

Conviction brings us to a place where we see our disobedience for what it is: rebellion. We stop rationalizing our behavior and start acknowledging what God already knows: we need His help.

God sees everything, which is why no matter how innocent we look we can't get away with sin. He also knows everything we've ever done and every act of disobedience we will commit in the future—and Jesus has already dealt with it on the cross. All we must do is acknowledge our sin and ask for forgiveness. Our Heavenly Father will take care of the rest.

We didn't scold Simon for breaking out of the back yard. He had tried to cover his tracks and he didn't know we knew what he had done. Frankly, I'm not even sure he thought it was wrong—after all, he is a dog.

As for us, instead of pretending we're innocent the next time we're caught red-handed, let's acknowledge our wrongdoing and ask for forgiveness.

Then we can come into the house guilt free.

***

Are you trying to fool God? Is He convicting you of anything?

"Our gospel came to you not simply with words but also with power, with the Holy Spirit and deep conviction (1 Thessalonians 1:5).

Chapter 22 – Unconditional Love

"All his life he tried to be a good person. Many times, however, he failed. For after all, he was only human. He wasn't a dog."—Charles M. Schulz

Unconditional Love. I see it every time I pull up the driveway to our house. The house sits on a hill, more than the length of a football field from the road. As Suki and I turn toward home, we can see Simon waiting on the front porch. His head pops up when he hears the car and soon he's bounding across the yard, barking an excited "hello."

I slow down as he approaches the car and he trots alongside escorting us into the garage as if he can't wait to tell us what he's been doing. Once the car doors open, Simon races from one side of the car to the other dividing his greeting between us. His whole body wiggles as he wags his tail and snuggles into Suki, then me to welcome us home. No matter how tired or grumpy I am, Simon's joy at seeing us always makes me smile.

I love coming home to a loving dog who's happy to greet me. Home is my place of safety and security. I can change into comfortable clothes and clear my head watching the birds soaring in the clouds and an occasional deer or rabbit.

I've lived in lots of places around the world and I know not every home is a place of refuge—or love. I can remember a time when coming home filled me with apprehension. I found excuses to stay away because I never knew what atmosphere was waiting behind the front door. I would hold my breath as I turned the knob trying to be invisible until I could make it to the relative safety of my room.

As a missionary I've lived in places that weren't comfortable or convenient. In Hawaii staff and students lived in dorm-like, open-air rooms with little or no privacy. In Thailand I slept on the floor of a bamboo hut with no electricity. I had to bathe fully dressed at the water pump at the center of the village. In the Philippines, we slept on old foam mats instead of traditional beds and took cold water bucket showers. In Haiti I retreated under my mosquito netting in the sweltering heat, hoping to fall asleep before the power went out.

So I thank God for the home God has given me in Tennessee—and for the faithful dog, who, rain or shine, snow or storm, always runs to meet me. It doesn't matter if we've been gone a few minutes or a few months. Simon's cheerful greeting is always the same. I think my enthusiastic canine companion is God's living illustration of unconditional love.

In the Bible, what we call "The Love Chapter" seems like an interruption in thought between two chapters about the gifts of the Spirit. This list of gifts in 1 Corinthians 12 is impressive: healing, miracles, prophecy, words of knowledge and discerning of spirits, to name a few.

When these gifts are on display, crowds gather. That's what happened when Jesus healed folks. It has continued when such gifts were manifested through folks like Smith Wigglesworth, Kathryn Kuhlman, Oral Roberts and Amy Semple McPherson.

Because the gifts of the Spirit are associated with power, it would be easy for us to develop a distorted view of what walking in the Spirit means. So to bring balance into our walk, Paul inserts a parenthetical note (the 13th chapter of 1 Corinthians) to remind us why the Holy Spirit gives us gifts—to demonstrate His love to the world.

Paul begins the chapter by warning us to check our motives. No matter how much power we have, if our motive to use it isn't love, it's worthless. He then follows up with a list of love's characteristics, before ending with the reminder that the gifts of the Spirit are temporary. (We won't need them in Heaven.) Only faith, hope and love will endure eternally.

Paul's dissertation on love is often used in weddings. However, in our rush to get to the "I do's" we've been known to mumble through the description of love. "Love is patient, love is kind. It does not envy, it does not boast, it is not proud. It does not dishonor others, it is not self-seeking, it is not easily angered, it keeps no record of wrongs. Love does not delight in evil but rejoices with the truth. It always protects, always trusts, always hopes, always perseveres. Love never fails."[14]

When I look at it, I know it's a list worth striving toward. I also know that without God's love working in me it's impossible achieve. I mean, who doesn't have a Naughty List on someone tucked away in a not-so-dusty trunk in the corner of his heart? And honestly, who can be patient all the time?

As I look down at Simon sleeping at my feet, I realize he is God's perfect illustration of unconditional love. He's content with who he is and he accepts who we are. He always protects, trusts, hopes and perseveres, without judging or trying to change us. (Although, I believe he would love us more if we gave him more goodies.)

1 John 4:8 says, "God IS love." (Emphasis mine) This means He doesn't have to work at patience or kindness or humility. His love never fails. He loves you and me—unconditionally. He didn't "fall" into love with us, so He can't "fall" out of love.

---

[14] 1 Corinthians 13:4-8.

Isn't it time we came home to His love? It's the safest, most peaceful refuge we'll ever know. And it's a perfect fit.

As we turn into the drive, I can see Him standing on the porch with a big smile on His face and His arms open wide waiting to welcome us home.

***

What is your understanding of unconditional love? How can you better show love to others?

And now these three remain: faith, hope and love. But the greatest of these is love (1 Corinthians 13:13).

Chapter 23 – I Need a Rub

"Petting, scratching, and cuddling a dog could be as soothing to the mind and heart as deep meditation and almost as good for the soul as prayer."—Dean Koontz

In 1995, Gary Chapman wrote the best-selling book, *The Five Love Languages: How to Express Heartfelt Commitment to Your Mate*.[15] Since then the concept of "love languages" has become a bona fide dimension of Christian counseling. According to Chapman, love is expressed in five different ways: receiving gifts, quality time, words of affirmation, acts of service and physical touch. Recognizing how we give and receive love is like having a tape measure in our relational tool belt—it can keep us from costly mistakes as we build our home.

---

[15] Gary Chapman, The Five Love Languages: How to Express Heartfelt Commitment to Your Mate, (Northfield Publishing, 1995).

While Chapman's book was written for humans, the same concept can be applied to our pets. Dogs give and receive affection from us too. It's easy to figure out the number one love language of dogs.

They're not too interested in gifts—unless it's food, and acts of service don't apply—unless, again, you're serving them food. While quality time with us is one expression of love they understand, it's primarily their gift to us. Words of affirmation are important to our pets in the moment, but they come in second on the love list. Like most dogs, Simon's primary love language is physical touch.

When he comes in after a romp in the yard, he wants a scratch behind his ears. In the evening when I sit in my chair, Simon flops down for a belly rub. When I get tired of rubbing him, he persistently puts his paw on my arm as if to say, "Hey! I'm still here and I need some love." Unless he's asleep and dreaming of some wonderful hunt through the woods, Simey is always ready to get off his comfortable pillow and come sit beside me to get a rub.

Researchers from the University of Florida created a series of tests to determine whether dogs preferred receiving vocal praise or praise from petting. Their overwhelming consensus was dogs prefer physical touch over verbal praise. While I have read their work and appreciate it, I think they probably could have saved a lot of time and money by simply asking anyone who owns a dog. "What's your dog's love language?"

As children many of us were taught not to pet a strange dog. And that's good advice. Some animals are leery of strangers. Others, even though they're normally calm pets, could bite if they're approached suddenly or without warning.

In his article, "Why do Dogs Like to Be Petted?"[16] Ben Team suggests some petting etiquette guidelines. For instance, we should never approach an unfamiliar dog to rub him—after all some mutts do bite strangers. We should also start slowly by offering an open hand, letting the pooch get a sniff of who we are. If he licks your hand or his tail wags, he's given you permission to pet him. And contrary to all our instincts, we shouldn't pat a dog on the head—according to research, they don't really like it. Our canine companions seem to prefer a good scratch behind the ears or under the chin—or, in Simon's case, a belly rub.

Why do dogs like to be petted? Here are a few "scientific" theories: It feels good—after all, who doesn't like a good massage? Stroking is also a way of bonding with the animal. Physical touch reduces a dog's heart rate and lowers his blood pressure. When I place my hand on Simon he relaxes, knowing I'm nearby. It tells him he's not alone and reminds him he's loved.

---

[16] Ben Team, "Why do Dogs Like to be Petted?" (February 5, 2017).

Of course, all those benefits work for the giver as well as the receiver. Studies have shown the bonding works both ways and the lower heart rate and blood pressure also applies to the petter. I've noticed that people enjoy scratching an animal almost as much as those furballs like being rubbed. You can't help but smile when you pet a pet.

We all need that kind of personal comfort from time to time. And while I might balk at being patted on the head, I'll never turn down a good hug. Touch is a critical part of our well-being. Studies in many orphanages have shown a lack of human touch can cause an increase in infant deaths. Those same surveys also showed children who suffered from touch deprivation achieved only half the height normal for their age.[17]

Hugs release a chemical called oxytocin, which not only lowers our blood pressure and heart rate, it helps us to feel connected. It eases stress and causes us to feel emotionally and psychologically supported—something we all need from time to time. The love language of touch gives life to us all.

The second love language Simon responds to is praise or words of encouragement. All we have to say is, "Good boy" to start his tail wagging like windshield wipers swishing back and forth on a rainy day.

---

[17] Debra Fulghum Bruce, How Can Lack of Touch Lead to Babies' Failure to Thrive?

The truth is, we all need consistent encouragement. Many of us regularly hear enough negative words from the world to last twenty lifetimes. Most of us tend to believe the critical words over the positive ones. The enemy knows this, so he works overtime to remind us of our shortcomings and failures. To counteract those discouraging words, we should be speaking words of encouragement to one another. It's a powerful tool in spiritual warfare.

In almost every one of his letters, Paul instructs the church to encourage one another. Whether we're going through a tough year or simply having a bad day, an encouraging word can lift our spirits and renew our energy—and most importantly, push back the lies of the devil.

Somehow scientists have figured out that we have 25,000 to 50,000 thoughts a day. The enemy wants us to turn all those thoughts inward instead of outward. He likes to remind us of our failures and shortcomings. When we're discouraged, the enemy stirs us into a downward self-focused spiral that can become like the ever-tightening funnel of a tornado, leaving nothing but brokenness behind.

No matter how discouraged we may be, God will use others to offer a positive idea or give a hug to reach out to us. Our failures and shortcomings are simply an invitation for God to step in and show us His love.

Personally, I've found the best way to pull myself out of the dumps is to encourage, serve or bless someone else. Once my focus turns outward, I get a more balanced perspective; I can see the value in others and I can become a Kingdom ambassador.

Another way to encourage others is to say, "Thank you." As a society, we're rapidly moving away from letter and note writing, and most of us prefer the speed of a computer over a time-consuming hand-written letter. However, every once in a while I'll receive a Thank You note in the mail and it always lifts my spirits. Saying, "Thank you" is an important way to honor others.

Note writers, encouragers and huggers invest in others, which is why people are attracted to them. They make us feel special because they have taken the time. In an electronic world that moves at the speed of light, it's easy to feel insignificant. That's why we all need some encouragement.

To put it in Simey's language, we simply don't get enough belly rubs, even when we roll over and beg. To put it in Paul's language, we need to practice encouraging others and being encouraged. I don't want to be the kind of dog owner or friend who has to be pawed to be reminded you're here.

So, what da ya say?

How about a little rub?

**

Do you need to be encouraged today? Or is there someone you know who needs a word of encouragement from you?

Finally, brothers and sisters, rejoice! Strive for full restoration, encourage one another, be of one mind, live in peace. And the God of love and peace will be with you (2 Corinthians 13:11).

Chapter 24 – The Problem of the Pack

"I wonder if other dogs think poodles are members of a weird religious cult."—Rita Rudner

Ever notice how like-minded folks stick together? Dogs do, too. It's called a pack—a group of hounds running together, acting as one unit. The group blindly follows their leader or Alpha dog. If Alpha growls, so does the gang. If Alpha chases something, the others race to catch up.

Simon's in a three-pack: him, Suki and I. We're still debating about who's Alpha. Simon thinks he is, which causes obedience problems in the family because Suki and I alternately also think we're Alpha. It's an ongoing negotiation.

The major issue isn't inside the house, it's outside. Our neighbors have four dogs. Individually, they're nice animals, but when they start thinking like a pack, they become a problem—not to us, to Simon. To them he's an outsider. When we hear snarling and barking followed by yelping and rustling, we know the pack has come into our yard and ganged up on Simon. I don't speak "Dog" so I'm not sure who starts the fight, but it's not a game.

The pack will circle around Simon nipping at him from opposite angles while he twirls in every direction trying to defend himself. Even though Simon is bigger and could eat a couple of them for a snack, the gang mentality has him cowering.

When we hear the scuffle, we charge outside to come to Simon's defense. We know better than to get in the middle of a dog fight and I'm not sure we could stop the brawl anyway, but shouting and waving our arms makes us feel better.

Simey has yelped his way home with battle-scarred ears more than once. But short of penning up every animal in the hood, there's not much we can do. After all, they are dogs.

Unfortunately, it's also human nature to run in packs. We tend to gravitate toward others with similar interests or beliefs. Today's trendy term is "tribes." Writers belong to a tribe. So do musicians, doctors, Christians, first responders, sports fans, teachers and teenagers—to name a few. (Sorry if I didn't mention yours.)

Each tribe is unique and has its own language and culture.

For example, I don't speak "Teenager." I've picked up a few phrases from them; however, I need a translator when they talk to one another. I don't even speak their second language: "Text." I'm so old school I text in full sentences without abbreviations. Like the two-fingered pecker at a keyboard, I'm trying to upgrade my skill, but "Text" is not my native tongue.

"Mechanic" is another language that's foreign to me. I don't know a crankshaft from a camshaft, or what a distributor is or why it needs a cap! (Is it having a bad hair day?) When my mechanic talks about my car, I nod and smile because I only understand about one-tenth of what he's saying. Please don't tell him.

Packs can be a good way to connect us to like-minded people. The problem with the pack is we begin to think our tribe is superior to all others. We believe we're better because we're more educated or richer or more in shape or less educated or poorer or foodies. God calls it pride.

It all begins with attitudes vocalized into words and finally magnified into actions. Before we know it, we gang up on "those other people," using the size, wealth or status of our group as moral justification to judge or intimidate anyone who looks, thinks or acts differently.

We've become a people divided. We splinter into packs and are offended if others oppose us on political or social issues. We've become increasingly aggressive and violent in our disagreement. We hurl rocks and insults, tear down statues, deface Synagogues and Nativity scenes and shout down speakers. It seems our packs have gone wild and the devil couldn't be happier.

As Christ-followers, our pack shouldn't look like the rest of the world. Unfortunately, sometimes we do. Like a pack of wild dogs, people who identified themselves as Christians have through the centuries made war on Jews and Muslims, drowned suspected witches, and oppressed people of different races and beliefs. Others have withdrawn from society into dangerous cults. Those were dark days in our history and prove we all can be deceived and swayed if we lose sight of Who our Alpha is.

The problem is, from a distance, it's hard to tell who's the leader of the pack. A mob on the street doesn't seem to have a leader, yet he's there. We won't find him with a stick in his hand busting out shop windows because by the time the action starts, he has stepped back into the shadows.

Like the director of a movie, Satan will always lead from the darkness behind the scenes. His language is slander and mistrust and his megaphone amplifies our doubts and fears. Once we believe his lies, all he has to do is shout, "Action" and we do his work for him.

Jesus, on the other hand, leads from love. He doesn't need a megaphone, He enlists His army with a whisper. His truth penetrates the heart and brings revelation, understanding and acceptance.

When He returns, Jesus will be on a white horse at the head of the crowd, not hiding in the shadows. He won't conscript His army through fear and intimidation because He has an all-volunteer army.

In Revelation, Jesus says, "I am the Alpha and Omega, the beginning and the end," which is a reference to the Greek alphabet: Alpha is the first letter and Omega is the last. In other words, He will lead the pack AND He will bring up the rear, leaving none of His volunteers broken and bleeding on the battlefield.

It's up to us to choose which leader to follow. We can put on a concealing hood, grab a stick and rail against those who are different, following a leader who slithers in a dark web. Or we can stand tall out in the open, following a Leader Who will lead the charge and His army at the same time.

The choice is mine. Once I decide, all I have to do is follow. And when it comes right down to it, isn't that what being in a pack is all about?

***

Who is your Alpha? What pack are you running with?

"I am the Alpha and the Omega," says the Lord God, "who is, and who was, and who is to come, the Almighty" (Revelation 1:8).

Chapter 25 – The Skunk

"Anybody who doesn't know what soap tastes like never washed a dog."—Franklin P. Jones

Do you spend much time thinking about air? I don't. I take it for granted. We can't see it, yet it's always around us. It supports the molecules and components we need to live. Our atmosphere also holds moisture and carries sound. It can be so still we don't know it's there or it can blow over the land with the strength to pick up a house. Oh, and one other thing about air—it carries smells.

I stood on the front porch and called for Simon. The warm air carried the fragrance of freshly mown grass. I saw the dog merrily trotting across the field in the light of the full moon. It was an idyllic scene out of a romance novel until...

Simon spun around, yelped and hightailed it to the front door. He looked like he was trying to run away from himself. We knew why as he charged into the house and our eyes began to water.

Skunk!

163

"Quick! Get him outside," Suki hollered.

I broke my own speed record as I grabbed his collar and herded the smelly mutt out back and slammed the door in his face. The pungent odor had already permeated the house. I was choking. I held my breath. It didn't help. We steeled ourselves for what was coming next. You can't ignore a face-to-face encounter with a skunk.

Owning dogs in the country ensures they'll meet lots of wild animals. Some are fun for a hound to chase like squirrels and rabbits; others can be downright dangerous like coyotes, snakes, bears and, Simon's nemesis, skunks. If a Pepe le Pew is in the hood, Simon is going after him.

Skunks are shy and try to avoid confrontation. However, when threatened, they will raise their tails and release a foul spray. Any adversary with half a brain would flee in the opposite direction the moment they see that tail go up.

The spray permeates everything it touches, and the longer it stays on something the harder it is to remove. Dog-skunk encounters rarely turn out well for the dog who usually ends up heading to the showers with his tail between his legs.

Giving Simon a bath after a skunk confrontation is more like a three-person "do-si-do" than a gentle soaking in the tub. Simey enjoys the scrubbing, but refuses to stay still. Suki keeps him tethered on the leash while I haul out the hose and soap. Then the circle dance begins: I wet one side. He backs away. Suki turns. Simon shifts. I circle to the other side. Simey twirls opposite. I soak the other side. Suki sidesteps the spray.

Then, we repeat—with soap.

Lots of odor eliminators claim to remove skunk smell. They range from home remedies to expensive commercial products, and we've tied many of them. One popular home treatment we applied was tomato juice. We ended up with a pink pup smelling of skunk who kept trying to lick the juice in his fur. We've also tested vinegar, baking soda and hydrogen peroxide solutions. We even bought some expensive professional odor remover for dogs. Guess what? None of them worked. No matter what product you use, only regular daily washings will successfully dilute the odor and, over time, get rid of the smell altogether.

So we begin the daily washing routine with the leash, the hose, the soap, the circle dance and a towel. We always end up soaked because Simon loves to shake before, during and after his bath.

Researchers say dogs can shake 70 percent of the water from their bodies in four seconds. Starting at the head and moving down the body, shaking at a speed of five spin cycles per second, animals can generate a force up to 70 times greater than gravity. The pressure is so strong dogs have to close their eyes to protect them. It's a God design so wild animals can dry off quickly and efficiently.

Simey shakes with vigor, but we still need the towel to deal with the remaining 30 percent. Then the towel also smells like skunk! It's a messy process that lasts for weeks—all because Simon stuck his nose into something he shouldn't have.

We, too,must deal with stinky left-overs from life issues. They often linger long after the event itself in our own lives and the lives of our children.

We got a note the other day from a friend saying, "I can't wait to tell you what God has done in my family!" We had been ministering to her and her husband for a while. Even though this precious couple had learned how to keep up appearances, there was still the faintest whiff of something sour in their relationship.

They were holding on to false beliefs from their childhood. Those ideas affected how they interacted with each other and their kids. Not only was the marriage in trouble, the whole family was fragmented. If left untreated, the brokenness of the parents could have carried down through their children to each successive generation. Yet, this couple kept fighting for their family, wash after wash, until the sourness was gone.

Some generational sins and lies have strong odors and need regular cleansing in order to get rid of the smell completely. Even when the original untruth is removed, the scent can remain. For instance, we may have repented of a sin and received forgiveness, but the feeling of guilt or shame can still cling to us. Some healings take time and repeated washings by the renewing of our minds. We may be clean, but our thoughts may still carry a whiff of skunk.

People are incredible survivors. Wounded people, if they shake hard enough, can expel 70 percent of their pain and get by. However, it's that left-over 30 percent that won't go away without God's help. He's the One holding the towel ready to finish the job.

That last 30 percent is the most painful to remove because it means acknowledging the truth: we've believed a lie that has hurt us and our children. Yet, God is gentle. He knows our hearts are as fragile as fine china so He tenderly wipes away our deep hurts with the softest of towels.

As the sour odor of pain disappears from our lives, God revives a fresh fragrance that sweetens the air around us and brings blessings to our next generations. When that new wind blows and the change comes, we simply have to say to someone, "I can't wait to tell you what God has done!"

All we have to do is stay away from the skunks.

***

Do you need some fresh air? Is there a remnant of a sour odor in your life?

"I will give you a new heart and put a new spirit in you; I will remove from you your heart of stone and give you a heart of flesh" (Ezekiel 36:26).

Chapter 26 – Going for a Ride

"Dogs feel very strongly that they should always go with you in the car, in case the need should arise for them to bark violently at nothing right in your ear."—Dave Barry

Simon comes galloping with high hopes every time he hears the grinding gears of the garage door opening. If he's in the house, the sound of car keys jingling will bring his head up from a sound sleep. All we have to do is say, "Go" to one another and he's halfway out the door. Our little adventurer is always ready to go for a ride.

Excitement vibrates through his whole body as he waits for me to open the back door of the pickup so he can jump in. Suki's truck is the dog-mobile and it suffers for it. Dog hairs have crept into every nook and cranny in the back of the cab creating an intricate paisley-like pattern on the black backseat cover where Simon sits. Nose "art" draws a line on the rear window telling the world how tall he is when he sits up. No matter how often Suki washes her truck, all it takes is one trip with

Simey-Boy for him to transform the back seat into his personal space.

Once he's in his spot behind the passenger's seat, he's content. He sits proudly like royalty being chauffeured through the streets of adoring fans. For a mile or two he surveys the world speeding past to determine our course, then he puts his head down and takes a nap. Simon's happy to doze off until he feels the car slow down or he hears the turn signal blinking. When he recognizes the cue, he'll pop his head up briefly to see where we are. Once he realizes we "aren't there yet," he settles back down on the seat to continue his snooze.

Somehow he can tell when we're headed to his favorite destination: the greenway, which is a paved path running along a small creek. When we are three or four blocks away, he sits up and resumes his post at the window. Two blocks out the whining starts and by the time we stop in the parking lot, he's a tail-wagging tongue-panting bundle of energy ready to bolt out the door.

His second favorite destination is the dump— probably because of the smells. Living in the country, we have to take our trash to a Convenience Center. On those days Simon is perched in his reserved spot on the backseat. The trip to the dump is usually a short one, but I think to Simey the smells are worth it.

The grocery run is next on Simon's fun-meter. Again, I think it's the allure of the smell. Perhaps somewhere in the back of his mind he's hoping we'll put the groceries in the backseat and leave him alone with a loaf of bread.

Of course, not every road trip leads to a fun destination. Sometimes we're taking him to the kennel or the vet's. Those are also places he can recognize from a distance. On these outings the whines aren't an overflow of excitement, they come from anxiety.

If Simon had his way, he'd schedule a road trip every day. He'd even drive if he could. But as smart as he is, he can't read the signs. His foot doesn't reach the gas pedal and his paws can't grasp the wheel. There have been times when Simon has hopped in the truck simply because the back door was open. He's seen no evidence of keys, nor have we put on coats or picked up our purses. The truck is simply sitting in the driveway.

The "ride" may end up being only a few feet back into the garage. He's content to lie down in the back seat and wait, completely trusting us and where we would take him. His desire to be with us is stronger than his fear of where we would go.

The story of the Israelites' road trip to the Promised Land is an excellent example of people who started out trusting their driver (Moses) to get them to their destination, but then wanted to take the wheel. Moses was confident because of his trust in God. His desire to be with Him overshadowed any fear of the future for himself or for the millions of former slaves following him in the

171

desert. As we know, the Israelites started whining when God's route was different than they expected. They wanted to go their own way, not trusting either Moses or God to lead them.

God told Moses, "Leave this place, you and the people you brought up out of Egypt, and go up to the land I promised on oath to Abraham, Isaac and Jacob, saying, 'I will give it to your descendants.' I will send an angel before you and drive out the Canaanites, Amorites, Hittites, Perizzites, Hivites and Jebusites. Go up to the land flowing with milk and honey. But I will not go with you, because you are a stiff-necked people and I might destroy you on the way." (Exodus 33:1-3)

Moses countered and said, "If your Presence does not go with us, do not send us up from here. How will anyone know that you are pleased with me and with your people unless you go with us? What else will distinguish me and your people from all the other people on the face of the earth?" (Exodus 33:15-16) Moses wasn't going anywhere without God.

The story ends with God relenting and reassuring Moses, saying, "I will do the very thing you have asked, because I am pleased with you and I know you by name." (Exodus 33:17)

Our desire to be with the Lord must be stronger than our fear of where we're going. Unless we're willing to trust Him and give Him control, we'll simply end up sitting in a motionless vehicle in the driveway. We won't be going anywhere.

Jesus is not the co-pilot of my car. He's the driver. So I have to ask myself, am I completely trusting when it comes to God taking the wheel of my life? Do I relax and let Him drive me where He wants to take me? Do I try to give Him directions from the poor perspective of the backseat? Or do I try to crawl in the front seat and steer a vehicle I'm not licensed, trained or able to operate?

When Simon gets in the truck, he doesn't know where we're going or how long we'll be gone—and he doesn't offer navigational advice. He's along for the ride. He settles in with confidence, contentment and anticipation every time we open the back door.

I think I hear some keys jingling and the garage door opening. A voice is saying, "Come on. Let's go." Are you ready to hop in?

***

Where are you putting your trust? Who's in the driver's seat of your life?

Let the morning bring me word of your unfailing love, for I have put my trust in you. Show me the way I should go, for to you I entrust my life (Psalm 143:8).

Chapter 27 – Marking Territory

"Why is it we want so badly to memorialize ourselves? Even while we're still alive. We wish to assert our existence, like dogs peeing on fire hydrants."—Margaret Atwood

Simon "goes" everywhere he goes. Suki and I often marvel at the size of his bladder and his ability to control it. On a mile-long trail he can leave his mark on twenty or more trees and bushes. However, he won't water every one simply because it's there. He sniffs around each potential target. He's picky.

He studies his objective from every angle. He approaches the unsuspecting plant from the left before turning and advancing from the right. He sniffs, and sniffs, and sniffs. Finally, if he deems it to be a worthy recipient, he lifts a leg to mark the territory—and misses the darn thing altogether!

When we're at home, Simey often marks the brick columns at the end of our driveway. If a stray pup happens by and leaves his scent behind, Simon rushes down the drive to cover up the interloper's smell. According to canine specialists a few drops of urine can tell other dogs about who's gone before, including the age, size and gender of the visitor and possibly even their social status.[18]

As if they were scanning the gossip column in the newspaper, reading territorial marking is how our furry friends learn what's happening in the neighborhood. Since smell is the hound's most dominant sense, it's an effective way to announce his presence to the four-legged community.

Long before Instagram and Twitter, a popular slogan announcing an American presence went viral—"Kilroy was here." The phrase was often accompanied by a cartoon drawing of a bald man with a big nose peering over a wall with only his eyes and fingertips showing. The graffiti was a humorous reminder of the presence of US military around the globe during World War II.

The funny face and slogan turned up in some outrageous places. There were reports of the cartoon appearing on the torch of the Statue of Liberty, inside the arch on the Arc de Triomphe in Paris, on the Marco Polo Bridge in China, on huts in Polynesia and on the George Washington Bridge in New York. By the end of World War II it seemed Kilroy had clearly been around the world and back.

---

[18] Adrienne Janet Farricelli, Understanding Dog Territorial Marking, (Pet-Helpful, October 18, 2016).

One of the boldest appearances was during the July 1945, Potsdam summit meeting of Harry Truman, Winston Churchill and Joseph Stalin. They had gathered to establish postwar order to Germany, which had surrendered unconditionally two months earlier. One day Stalin reportedly used their private bathroom, and came out demanding, "Who is Kilroy?"

In December of 1946, the *New York Times* ran a contest to discover the origin of the Kilroy phenomenon. A welding inspector at the Bethlehem Steel shipyard named James L. Kilroy was credited with starting the craze. Inspectors would mark the section inspected with a small chalk mark, but when Kilroy would finish an inspection he would write the phrase "Kilroy was here." The slogan became a common sight in the shipyard, and when steelworkers enlisted in the service, they began to reproduce the slogan wherever they went. The popular cartoon brought a moment of levity to a dark time in our history.[19]

I think there's a bit of Kilroy and Simon in all of us. Whether it's a business, an inheritance or a set of ethics, we want to leave a legacy. For many, children are our legacy. Others "mark" their place by making a movie, constructing a building, recording an album or painting a picture. Some write a novel, break a school record or invent

---

[19] The Straight Dope, What's the origin of "Kilroy was here"?, (August 4, 2000).

something—all ways of saying we were here. One day we will all stand before God and answer the question, "How did you invest the life I gave you?" Kingdom marks are eternal but often obscure when it comes to world recognition.

My friend Gregg Scott never built a bridge or an empire but he did make a significant Kingdom investment. Born in New Zealand in 1950, he married, had kids and built a successful business. Then he met Jesus and followed His call into Youth With A Mission.

He shared the love of Jesus with folks in Indonesia, the Philippines, Ukraine and the United States. At the age of 56 he moved his family to Montana where he continued his mission work in Tanzania and Bali drilling wells and distributing medical supplies to villages. The world took little notice when Gregg died at age 67. The people who loved him grieved but, more importantly, Heaven took notice. Gregg had invested his life well.

As I look around, the only eternal things I see are people. Scripture tells us even though we were created, we will exist forever, either with Jesus or without Him. Consequently, if I want to leave a lasting mark, I need to focus on people.

If we put our energy into others, the next obvious question is *what* should we be investing? Time? Money? Knowledge? How about depositing everlasting values into everlasting beings?

As Christ-followers, we could extend love to the loveless, hope to the despairing and truth to the one seeking answers. We can offer joy to the sorrowful one, peace to the one in turmoil, kindness to the discouraged one and faith to the lost one.

Kingdom investments can be small—an offering to one person at a time. They can look like a smile to the tired mechanic putting air in your tires, a kind word to the neighbor you pass on the sidewalk, a hug to an overworked mother or time spent listening to a friend's troubles.

We don't have to sniff around for unusual places to leave our mark. Chalk and dog scents eventually get washed away.

Eternal things—well—they last forever.

***

Where are you investing yourself? Will your investment wash away over time or will it be eternal?

Praise be to the God and Father of our Lord Jesus Christ! In his great mercy he has given us new birth into a living hope through the resurrection of Jesus Christ from the dead, and into an inheritance that can never perish, spoil or fade. This inheritance is kept in heaven for you (1 Peter 1:3-4).

Chapter 28 – Is Today the Day?

"The greatest fear dogs know is the fear that you will not come back when you go out the door without them."—Stanley Coren

As silly as it seems, we hide the suitcases from Simon when we're going on a trip. The sight of our travel gear sets off his anxiety so we pretend all is normal. We watch our words and pack behind closed doors. We have been known to distract him one at a time in the back yard while the other loads the suitcases into the car in the front.

He still figures it out. He knows we're leaving.

Canines are social animals. Unlike cats who look forward to alone time in the house, dogs can become depressed when their masters are gone. While they don't understand time as we do, they adapt to our daily 8:00 to 5:00 workday routines. Whenever we leave, our furry friends wait for us.

That leads us to the story of Hachi, a dog who became a national hero in Japan. Hachi was an Akita dog who was adopted by Eizaburo Ueno, a professor at Tokyo University. The two soon were inseparable. Hachi escorted Eizaburo to the Shibuya Train Station each day for work and returned in the evening to meet his owner when he came home. Whether it was a day trip or a longer business trip, Hachi met every train at the station until his friend returned.

One morning his owner boarded the train as usual, but didn't arrive home that evening. Eizaburo had died unexpectedly at work from a cerebral hemorrhage. Meanwhile Hachi waited at the station. When his friend didn't get off the train that day, Hachi returned the next, and the next, and the next. Though the family's gardener adopted Hachi, he continued to meet the train every day. Through rain and snow he would sit for hours, patiently longing for his beloved Eizaburo. *Is today the day he will come home to me?*

Year after year Hachi continued his daily vigilance on the platform. He became known as "The Faithful Dog" and as his story spread throughout Japan, people would stop at the Shibuya Station to give him treats.

Almost ten years after his owner died, Hachi lay his head down on the platform and closed his eyes for the final time. He died waiting at the place where he had last seen his lifelong friend.

If you were to visit the Shibuya Station in Tokyo today you would be greeted by a statue of Hachi, sitting with his head cocked to one side faithfully watching for his beloved owner and friend to come home.[20]

Dogs are loyal. Their devotion to us displays a depth of love we rarely see from other animals. Personally, I think God created man's best friend with a unique dedication to their owners for a reason—to illustrate His love and devotion to us.

We get teary-eyed and marvel at a dog's commitment to his master, yet we shrug off the same faithfulness from our Father God. Can you imagine God waiting for you to come home every day like Hachi waited for his master? Jesus tells a story in Luke 15:11-32 that perfectly illustrates God's faithfulness. A wealthy man had two sons. The younger son was tired of working on the farm. City lights and glamour were calling his name (my version). The young man went to his dad and demanded his inheritance, so the gracious father divided his estate between his sons. The younger took his half, left home and blew through the cash. In no time he went from living high on the hog to living with the hogs. He longed for his former life on the farm, remembering the lavish meals and his comfortable bed (again, my version).

Verse 20 continues: "So he got up and went to his father."

"But while he was still a long way off, his father saw him and was filled with compassion for him;

---

[20] Maria, The Amazing And True Story of Hachiko The Dog, (October 15, 2018).

he ran to his son, threw his arms around him and kissed him."

"The son said to him, 'Father, I have sinned against heaven and against you. I am no longer worthy to be called your son.'

"But the father said to his servants, 'Quick! Bring the best robe and put it on him. Put a ring on his finger and sandals on his feet. Bring the fattened calf and kill it. Let's have a feast and celebrate. For this son of mine was dead and is alive again; he was lost and is found.' So they began to celebrate."

What impresses me in this story is the wealthy landowner saw his son while he was still a long way off and ran to him. Many a father would have washed his hands of this rebellious son, or perhaps hired a detective to find him or have servants keep watch for him.

If I may blend the two stories, like Hachi, every morning and evening the father in this parable would go to the train station. He would scan the crowds longing to see his son's face in the throng. The next day he would do the same, month after month, and year after year, rain or snow—looking, longing, wondering. *Is today the day he will come home to me?*

The story we call The Prodigal Son is one of a string of stories Jesus tells to illustrate how God has chosen to relate to us. He has given us free will, which means He won't stop us from getting on the train and heading off to parts unknown. He knows our tendency to get lost and squander His blessings, yet he doesn't try to shield us from consequences of our choices. He will, however, always be waiting on the platform for us to return.

In March of 2015, on the 80th anniversary of his death, another statue of Hachi was unveiled on the campus of the University of Tokyo. It's a rendering of the joyous scene of Hachi jumping up to greet Eizaburo as he returns home. In the sculpture the two devoted and faithful friends are finally reunited and the overflowing joy shines on both their faces at the long-awaited reunion. Even if it's only in the imagination of the sculptor, the story has come full circle. Eizaburo and Hachi are together at last.

Is your suitcase packed to leave or are you coming home? Either way, I promise you God is scanning the faces in the crowd, looking for yours.

***

Have you slipped away from God? Isn't it time to return home?

"But while he was still a long way off, his father saw him and was filled with compassion for him; he ran to his son, threw his arms around him and kissed him" (Luke 15:20).

Chapter 29 – The Tumor

"Old dogs, like old shoes, are comfortable. They might be a bit out of shape and a little worn around the edges, but they fit well."—Bonnie Wilcox

According to the old saying, two things are inevitable and unchangeable: death and taxes. I've paid my taxes so let's talk about death.

Our little Simey has a tumor but he doesn't know it. Last November we felt a small lump on his left side above his hip so we took him to Dr. Amy. After a biopsy she quietly confirmed what we suspected. It was a malignant mass.

"It's slow growing," she said.

That fact didn't stop the stabbing pain in our hearts, which now registered on our faces.

With sympathy she explained, "We can operate and try to remove it, but this type of tumor has spidery-like tentacles and it's impossible to get it all, so it will eventually come back."

We didn't know what to say.

187

"We could also give him chemotherapy or radiation," she added. "It might prolong his life a little."

"Is he in any pain now?" Suki asked.

"No."

"Will he be?"

"It's hard to tell," she replied.

With tears in our eyes, we left her office and took Simon for a romp on the greenway—one of his favorite things to do. Like wringing out a dishrag, sadness squeezed our hearts as we watched him gleefully sniff every bush and mark as many trees as he could. He explored. We cried.

Simon is 13-years-old, which is old for a large dog. He's closer to the end of his romping days than the beginning, but then so am I.

When we're young and healthy we don't think about death, yet it's always lurking in the background. Death came into the Garden of Eden with sin and it will always be a part of life on this planet. No one can cheat it.

However, when we hear the word "tumor," Death steps out from behind the curtain, bullies his way forward and stops us in our tracks. One day we will have to look Death in the eye.

Even our beloved Simey-Boy will face him.

As Simey's tumor grows, we can see the curtain beginning to peel back a bit. So we're doing everything we can to make his senior years as joyful as his puppy days. I'd say Simon has had a pretty good life. (Of course, if you were to ask him, he'd probably say he hasn't had enough treats.)

He was adopted by people who loved him. He always had a roof over his head and a bowl of food nearby. He has had the freedom to chase squirrels and rabbits (and skunks) in the country and he has explored new territory on camping trips, hiking trails and rides in the truck.

He has had great fun, yet he has never been simply a taker. Simon has also given back. Waiting on the front porch for us to come home, he tells us we've been missed. The pup proclaims his love as he joyfully barks a welcome and escorts Suki and me up the driveway. He keeps us company as he sits nearby on his pillow and brings laughter as he rolls around in the snowmaking doggie snow angels. Simey teaches us trust when he lets us clean a cut or bandage a bleeding ear. He's our guardian and protector and has brought laughter and love into our lives in a way no person could.

Simon knows his position in the family and doesn't try to be anything else. He celebrates his life with fresh joy and anticipation with each new day. He knows he has a job to do and he does it. His assignment: be the dog. He has done it well.

Our four-legged boy doesn't brood about the past and he doesn't fret about the future. When he sleeps, he's worry-free. When he barks, it's with abandon. And when he loves, it's with all the loyalty and devotion he has.

189

Can we say the same about ourselves? Do we embrace the richness of each moment or do we let our past weigh us down like a heavy suit of armor? Are we aware of the beauty around us or does worry distort our vision like looking through scratched sunglasses?

Are we loving well? Do we greet each day with new mercies and anticipation for what's ahead? Are we making the most of every opportunity or frittering away our time?

Only the Lord knows the number of our days. Peter, in quoting Isaiah, reminds us our time is short. "All people are like grass, and all their glory is like the flowers of the field; the grass withers and the flowers fail, but the word of the Lord endures forever." (1 Peter 1:24-25) God has given each of us the gift of time—24 hours every day—no more, no less. How we use our time matters.

There's a great line from one of my favorite musicals, *Man of La Mancha*. Miguel de Cervantes, author of Don Quixote, is a character in the play and on his final exit says, "I've been a soldier and a slave. I've seen my comrades fall in battle or die more slowly under the lash in Africa. I've held them in my arms at the final moment. These were men who saw life as it is, yet they died despairing. No glory, no brave last words, only their eyes, filled with confusion, questioning 'Why?' I do not think they were asking why they were dying, but why they had never lived."[21]

Simply because we're breathing, doesn't mean we're living. To truly live is to be in Christ. The abundant life, which Jesus spoke of in John 10:10, was life purchased by His death and resurrection. It's a life that not only restored our broken relationship with God, but gave us eternal life.

The question of Jesus' death is one we all must grapple with. Our response to it will determine forever how we choose to live. With Jesus as our Savior we no longer have to fear Death, so we're free to focus on the living.

Simon moves a little slower now. He sleeps more than before and it's harder for him to shift from sitting to standing. He won't be here forever, but he's making the most of his life one day at a time. Simon won't leave a lasting mark on the world, but he will leave one on my heart.

As Simon has done, let's live well.

***

What is your response to the cross? Are you making the most of your days?

Teach us to number our days, that we may gain a heart of wisdom (Psalm 90:12).

---

[21] Dale Wasserman, Man of La Mancha, (lyrics by Joe Darion, music by Mitch Leigh, 1965).

Chapter 30 – The Master's Voice

"Man is a dog's idea of what God should be."—
Holbrook Jackson

Simon can be bribed to come to you if you
have a treat in your hand. That's about the only
way a stranger can lure him to their side. However,
if I call his name, he comes running—most of the
time. He has spent his life with me and he knows
the sound of my voice.

When I was a child, I loved Elvis. I would shake
my leg and curl my lip and sing "You Ain't Nothin'
But a Hound Dog" over and over. I had a record
player and a stack of Elvis 45's that I would play for
hours. Of course it took hours because with 45's
you had to change the record with each song. (Life
was slower then.)

I loved the colorful array of record labels, but
my favorite was the distinctive RCA Victor
trademark. It had a shiny black background with a
picture of a white dog sitting by a gramophone
with his ear inclined to the horn.

The image was taken from an 1899 painting by Mark Barraud of his family pet, Nipper. In the 1970s the image was fashioned into a bronze statue and awarded to artists who sold more than 100,000 recordings. The title of the statue was "His Master's Voice."

All pups know their master's voice. Performer and humorist Will Rogers once said, "If you think you're a person of some influence, try ordering someone else's dog around." Hound dogs aren't impressed with clothing, money, titles or position. They don't respond with any preference to deep voices or squeaky ones. And while they may love everyone in the family, they only have one master. His or hers is the voice that matters.

Can you see where this one is heading? As Christ-followers we, too, have only one Master: Jesus, and He won't share His Lordship. Some people want to add Jesus to their existing belief system in order to "hedge their bets," thinking if one ideology doesn't work, the other will be their insurance against Hell. Yet Jesus won't be treated that way. He even says, "I am the only way to the Father."[22] According to Him, either He is God or He's not. There's no mushy middle ground.

If He's God, He can't be ignored. If He's our Master, saying, "No" isn't possible. If we say, "No," He's not our Master. If we call Him, "Master," we can't say, "No." Because He created us He has

---

[22] John 14:6.

authority to direct our lives, yet He doesn't. He's not a puppeteer pulling strings through the clouds to make us dance to His tune. He's a God who wants a relationship with us.

Christ-followers recognize and obey Jesus' voice. Four voices are clamoring for attention in our heads. They include our own voice, the voices of others, the voice of the enemy and God's voice. Learning to recognize which voice is speaking makes our lives as Christ-followers much simpler.

The first two voices are easy. The voice of others is simply the things other people have said to us, which can be good or bad. Our own voice is usually the selfish voice in our heads wanting things "our way."

The enemy's voice is vehement and demanding like a bully. His strategy is to be the loudest voice, and it has proven quite effective through the centuries. Another way to recognize the enemy's voice is to notice his vocabulary. He uses words like "always," "never," "enough," and "more"—words that can't be measured. For instance, he might say, "You always waste time. You don't study enough. You will never triumph."

God, on the other hand, wants us to succeed. So He sets goals that we can reach. For instance, He might say, "Read your Bible ten minutes each day." That's something you can do and it's measurable. If we miss a day, God doesn't get mad. He says, "Start again tomorrow."

Although His voice can be loud like thunder and rushing water, God doesn't usually talk to His children like that. Our Master's voice is quiet and gentle—thus the need to lean in to listen. The drawing near to hear Him is by design. Have you ever had to move closer to someone to catch what they're saying? The closeness brings intimacy and intentionality. God wants us to be deliberate and focused when we meet with Him. He won't compete with the computer, television, your video game or your phone. After all, He's God and He sets the rules.

Many claim they've never heard God speak, but that's not true. Scripture tells us God speaks to all mankind through His creation, so no one has an excuse. (Romans 1:20) God also speaks through the Bible, through the Holy Spirit, through our conscience, our circumstances—even Simon. All we need to do is incline our ears.

Listening and hearing are not the same. I can do nothing and hear sounds around me. Listening, on the other hand, is an action verb. It means to give one's attention, to take notice of and act on what someone says. The very act of listening requires my focus, and that's how I get to know God better.

Do you remember the first thing God said to you? I do. He said, "I love you." Those three words rocked my world—more than when my parents said it, or when my boyfriend said it, or my ex-husband or anyone else. When God, Who made the gazillion stars and galaxies and creatures and plants on the earth, bent down close to me and said those words, it changed everything.

I couldn't imagine a God that big could be interested in an insignificant human like me. But He whispered my name—*my name.* Then He leaned in close and made it personal. "I love you." To me, that was a God worth getting to know.

Like Nipper on the RCA label, Simon may be "nothin' but a hound dog," but he's my hound dog. He spends his days with me and he recognizes my voice. As for you and me, the more time we spend with Jesus, the easier it will be for us to know His voice, too.

Why don't you join me by the gramophone? We can incline our ears together. Jesus has something important to say to you. I promise you'll recognize The Master's Voice. It's the one saying, "I love you."

***

Do you need to take time to sit by your Master? What is Jesus saying to you?

My sheep listen to my voice; I know them, and they follow me (John 10:27).

One Last Thought

Thank you for joining Suki, Simon and me on our adventures and misadventures in the hills of Tennessee. Once again, God has reminded me that all creation reveals His glory. He has new lessons to teach us in every aspect of our lives. All we have to do is take some time to look for Him. As I've shared these stories, I've made a few discoveries along the way. Some have brought a smile to my heart, others have brought a tear; however, He has met me at both ends of the spectrum. My prayer is that He has met you as well.

Till we meet again.

Blessings,
M. J. Miller

Other books by M. J. Miller:
Life Lessons from the Hive

Available on Amazon

Made in the USA
Coppell, TX
11 November 2019

11263012R00120